Tom Matte's

Tales from the

BALTIMORE RAVENS SIDELINE

Tom Matte
with
Jeff Seidel

Sports Publishing L.L.C.
www.SportsPublishingLLC.com

Director of production: Susan M. Moyer
Acquisitions editor: Robert Snodgrass
Project manager: Kathryn R. Holleman
Developmental editor: Dean Miller
Dust jacket design: Heidi Norson
Imaging: Heidi Norson and Kerri Baker
Copy editor: Cynthia L. McNew

ISBN: 1-58261-754-6

Printed in the United States of America.

Sports Publishing L.L.C.
www.SportsPublishingLLC.com

To my wife, Nadine, who has been there and put up with me through it all. Thankfully, she's a better writer than I am. Also to my very patient kids, Zach and Kara. Hey, guys, I'm finally off the computer now. — *J.S.*

To my wife, Judy, who has supported me and been there for so many things during my football life. Also for my children, Roland and Kate, who understood why their dad had to travel so much. — *T.M.*

CONTENTS

FOREWORD

I think the Baltimore Ravens have meant everything to the sports fans of this city. The city took a vicious shot to the body and was down on its knees after the Colts left in the middle of the night. It wasn't just losing the Colts, but having to go those 12 years without a team; it was sort of like we had to keep asking for a date and getting turned down for the prom.

We saw teams go into Carolina and Jacksonville and the league kept saying, no, we don't want to go to Baltimore. But that's why getting a team back meant so much; the fans felt we were whole again. I think, suddenly, we could stick our chests out again. The city took great pride in having a team and meaningful Sundays again.

One thing I (and Baltimore fans) won't forget was interviewing commissioner Paul Tagliabue at the NFL meeting where the league passed on Baltimore for the second time. I interviewed him after his news conference, and my question was, well, Baltimore sold out the NFL preseason game between the Saints and Dolphins, the state's stadium deal is set, so after this latest rejection, what do you tell the people of Baltimore? And that's when he said, "We can't tell the people of Baltimore what to do. Maybe they'd be better off building a plant or a museum."

Not exactly what hurting Baltimore fans wanted to hear that night. I guess it did lead to those popular T-shirts that read "Hey, Tagliabue, how do you like our museum?"

Art Modell, he was the guy that brought football back. That will be his legacy in this town. He gave us the ball back after it was ripped out of our arms for 12 years. When Art came, it was more than just getting the game back. In a perfect world, Art's still in Cleveland and Baltimore gets an expansion team named the Colts with horseshoes on the helmet, but that wasn't the deal.

Art Modell was a legitimate owner who was linked with most of the greats in the game; he brought a storied franchise to a football-starved community and left the Browns colors and history where they belonged. From day one, he moved into our community and just jumped in head-first. It wasn't Bob Irsay, who flew in on game day, often embarrassed himself and the franchise and flew back to Illinois. I think most Baltimore fans embraced the new owner, but there were a lot of people who weren't comfortable with the circumstances that brought Baltimore its new team. But if they really look at the facts, they'll see he did what he had to do. Art Modell, for what he and his family invested in the city of Cleveland, didn't want to move out of there, but circumstances, many which were dictated by Cleveland politicians, forced the move.

The Ravens' Super Bowl run was the thing that cemented the team's love affair with the area. There were a lot of people who were skeptical about accepting the new team. They had one eye on the team, but they weren't buying tickets, they didn't like the way we got the team; after all, Johnny U wasn't the quarterback and "they weren't the Colts." I think that season kind of pulled many of them in. Right then many felt that this is "my" team. The Ravens were suddenly theirs, a vital fabric that unites us and makes a community. Half the kids in school were dressed in purple, half the cars on the Beltway had Ravens flags flying. Everything seemed to change.

I think that the Ravens can be as big as the Colts were here, but they've only played eight years in Baltimore. They've won a Super Bowl; the stadium is full for every home game. The state built a state-of-the-art stadium to showcase the team. I just think there needs to be more time to compare them with the legacy of the Colts. The Colts were here and were a vital part of the NFL bursting on the national scene.

When the Colts started in the 50s, the NFL was second to college football nationally. The 1958 championship game with the Giants wasn't "the greatest game ever played" but it was likely the most important game ever played. National TV, New York, Unitas, the first overtime thriller all helped ignite the tremendous success the game enjoys today. It's hard to compare the Ravens' popularity with Baltimore's love affair with the Colts just yet because of the longevity factor, but I don't think the passion for the Ravens is any less. Ray Lewis and Todd Heap are just as popular today as John Unitas and Raymond Berry were 45 years ago.

That's what Tom and Jeff look at in this book: a bunch of stories that will give the fans who have that passion for the Ravens even more to be interested in. The bottom line—it gives you great fans more inside information, more memories, and hopefully some smiles as you read about the team you love.

SCOTT GARCEAU
Ravens Radio Play-by-Play Announcer

ACKNOWLEDGMENTS

We kept this a pretty low-key and simple project from the start, basically framing the book by having numerous long conversations in Tom's office and again over the phone.

But we still owe a lot of thanks to several people and organizations. First, of course, thanks to the Ravens and their great PR staff. Kevin Byrne, Francine Lubera, Chad Steele and Marisol Renner have been huge helps to both of us countless times over the years. Since Jeff writes for several different publications and Tom is the color analyst on the team's radio broadcasts, they're always asking this group for something—and they'll usually come through.

Thanks to photographers Mitchell Layton, Phil Hoffmann and Stuart Zolotorow, who generously gave us carte blanche to look at their Ravens pictures and also use them. If a picture is worth a thousand words, then we've got about a million words in this book.

Also thanks to the people we talked to for advice on this project. Scott Garceau, Howard Gartner, Randy Gartner, Dave Ginsburg, Bruce Laird, Josh Land, Andy Levin, Stan Rappaport, Neil Rubin, Rich Soherr, Josh Smith, John Ziemann, If we forgot anyone, no offense intended.

A big thank you also goes to our editor at Sports Publishing, Dean Miller. He came on to the team later in the game but did an absolutely fabulous job of giving us direction and order. The finished product wouldn't have come close to looking like it does if not for his efforts.

And for both of us, thanks to the people around us who've helped in other ways. To Jeff's mom, Elaine Seidel, this might be the first sports book she's ever read. Hope she likes it. I'm sorry Dad isn't here to see it, but I'm sure he'd love it. To Jeff's in-laws, Leroy and Muriel Handwerger, thanks for all of their support in so many ways. To Tom's family, who've always been so supportive through the last 50 years of football, either playing or broadcasting. The game is still going, and he still loves it and loves that his family has been there.

Chapter 1

THE FRONT OFFICE:
ART MODELL, STEVE BISCIOTTI, AND MANAGEMENT

Finding the Talent

The Baltimore Ravens have earned a lot of respect throughout the NFL in the last few years for their defense. But they might have earned even more respect for the way they've been able to find talent in all kinds of places.

In addition to Ozzie Newsome, the team's executive vice president and general manager, Phil Savage, George Kokinis, Eric DeCosta, and James Harris (now with Jacksonville) have played a large role in helping the Ravens find all kinds of talent from all kinds of places. All three were promoted before the 2003 season after helping the team continue to dig up a large number of strong players.

Savage became a member of the Cleveland franchise in 1991 before it moved to Baltimore. He started as a coach's assistant and kept moving up until earning a promotion to director of player personnel before the 2003 season.

Savage has been a driving force in the team's very successful drafts, which included picking star players like Ray Lewis, Jonathan Ogden, Peter Boulware, Todd Heap, Jermaine Lewis and others.

"I'm an original Raven, and I'm proud of that," Savage said. "I believe we have the ingredients in this organization to win at the highest level. I'm confident we'll compete for championships in the years to come."

Kokinis then became the pro personnel director. Savage had done that job for the last seven years, and everyone moved up when James Harris left the Ravens to go to Jacksonville for the 2003 season.

DeCosta then took Savage's old job as director of college scouting. Savage had been in that job for the past seven years.

"I believe in promotion from within whenever possible," Newsome said. "That helps your continuity and productivity. We know each other well, and that results in better players for the team. The personnel group we have right now is basically the same set of evaluators we had for our first draft [1996] when we selected three Pro Bowl players—[Jonathan] Ogden, Ray [Lewis] and Jermaine [Lewis]."

Newsome also said that the promotions would continue to help Savage, DeCosta, and Kokinis in numerous ways.

"For Phil, this promotion gets him more involved in the pro side, plus he'll increase his work in contract negotiations and have more daily contact with our coaches and the evaluation of our players," Newsome said. "George and Eric worked hard for these promotions. They are well respected around the NFL, and they are key players and have been key players in our search for more talent on the team."

Other teams already had started courting Savage for general manager-type jobs. He nearly took a front office job with Jacksonville before the 2003 season, but negotiations there broke down. He also interviewed for a similar job with Miami that Dan Marino later took—and then resigned from just a few weeks later. Harris went to Jacksonville as vice president of player personnel, and the Jaguars also brought in Jack Del Rio as coach. Del Rio was a former Baltimore assistant coach under Billick.

Jonathan Ogden, one of three Pro Bowlers selected during Ozzie Newsome's first draft in Baltimore. (Photo by Mitchell Layton)

Matte's Musings on the Salary Cap and How Change Affects Things

"That's why the league is so balanced now. Once you get up there and you get the real good football players and they demand the kind of money that they want, you can just pass them on if you want. If somebody else has less of a salary cap and cleaned house, they can pick some people up like the Ravens did because they cleaned house after 2001. I think they're probably the best off in the salary cap that there is. They kept it down there low and can go out and pick up some players I think are going to enhance this ball club so that they'll be in the playoffs again next year, except I think they'll go a lot farther. I think they have a chance to go all the way.

"They cleaned house. It's league rules. What are you going to do? You get rid of Sam Adams, you get rid of Michael McCrary, Tony Siragusa retires, you put Jamie Sharper on the expansion list, you get rid of Shannon. The Ravens got rid of some guys who had contracts that would affect the cap there. So they cleaned house, and when you have a scouting group like Ozzie and Phil Savage and the rest of the guys who work with them, they find the players who come back in. They've done such a great job with finding the players like Marques Douglas, Ed Hartwell, Kelly Gregg, Will Demps. Cornell Brown, the linebacker. Defensively they're just great. Edwin Mulitalo, where the hell do you find him from? He's great on the offensive line. Casey Rabach has been good there, too, and I think will develop. I was really sad when wide receiver Brandon Stokley left. He was a great receiver, but he was a little injury-prone. But what a competitor. If I could make up a team of about 50 guys of that kind of caliber, I could win championships with kids like that.

"The way they've turned it around in two years has been absolutely phenomenal as far as I'm concerned. Even with the 7-9 record in 2002, if they don't lose the last two games in there, they're 9-7 and could have gone to the playoffs. They lost those games by a total of four points. How can you be that competitive? Again, it comes back to the fact that Billick has these guys ready in November and December, when you have to be healthy. Even with the purge that was made, getting rid of the high salary cap people, he still makes these guys competitive. That comes down from the leadership from the coaching staff. They even lost Ray Lewis for most of the season. Hartwell steps up and plays All-Pro for the rest of the season for them. This is a kid who should be getting more respect than what he's getting. He's a quiet kid who always goes out and gets the job. Those kinds of guys are the ones they're trying to keep under contract. What you want to do is—you have the extra money now—is you know what kind of players these guys are and you've got to bring them back, especially on defense. You've got to get them signed up somehow. You want to keep that unit intact somehow. You really do.

"There probably won't be too many changes on defense. If there's more than one or two changes, I'd be amazed. It's a unit that works together. They've got a lot of pride. But you have to concentrate on the offense. What you have to concentrate on is the receiving corps. You have to concentrate on game plans. I think you really have to go back and review what happened this year and chart it out and say here's what we did and how we can be more successful. Billick is smart enough to do that. I don't have any questions about his study habits and charting himself. My feelings still are that you have to be able to utilize the backs coming out of the backfield. You have to be able to run pass patterns, individual pass patterns and combination pass patterns that you set up during a game that you want to use. I can remember when I played going back with Unitas…Jimmy Orr, the wide receiver, would say, 'I've got the corner pattern all set up. He'll take the bite to the inside, I'll straighten it out and then just lay it out in the corner for me.' It's a timing pattern.

But you have to work on those timing patterns and you have to work on the steps, and you have to work on the release times."

Ozzie's Talk

Many big-time sports executives are big-time people who live for and love being in the spotlight. But Ozzie Newsome is not that way. Here's a story that demonstrates what's important to Newsome:

The Baltimore Sun asked him to speak at its June 2003 luncheon honoring its high school Athletes of the Week for the past school year. Several of the writers who covered high school sports—and some other things—sat at a table right in front of the podium.

The Ravens were running some type of mini-camp that week, which left Newsome and his friends very busy. But he snuck out from the team's headquarters and drove the 20 minutes over to where the banquet was being held in Towson.

He quietly slid in through the side door while the banquet was going on—very few saw him—and quickly sat down at the table with the writers.

"Uh-oh, now I'm in trouble," Newsome said with a laugh.

He then quietly talked and laughed with everyone for several minutes before going up to give his speech. Now sports figures often give talks that discuss their favorite subject—themselves. But Newsome gave a stirring speech that had everyone, including the writers, paying rapt attention.

He exhorted the kids to always do their best and keep working hard to reach their goals and believe in what they were doing. And he did it in such a way that people were buzzing about it afterwards.

When the speech was over, Newsome came back to the table and quietly sat down, accepting congratulations all around.

Newsome sat for a moment or two and then quietly slid out through the same side door through which he entered minutes before. He could have told the paper that because it was during the mini-camp, showing up would be impossible. Instead, Newsome squeezed a high school banquet into the schedule of an NFL executive.

"You Have to Have a Plan"

Newsome was promoted to general manager and executive vice president in 2002—and it was easy to understand why.

Just take a look at the team's top draft picks during the organization's time in Baltimore. Jonathan Ogden, Ray Lewis, Peter Boulware, Duane Starks, Chris McAlister, Jamal Lewis, Travis Taylor, Todd Heap, Ed Reed, Terrell Suggs and Kyle Boller. Each one has played a major role in the Ravens' success.

Newsome has helped the Ravens achieve close to a perfect record with first-round draft choices. He and the Ravens have had one of the NFL's best records for mid- and lower-round picks who have helped the Ravens become one of the league's better teams in recent years. They've also done almost as well with free agents. Shannon Sharpe, Trent Dilfer, Sam Adams, Tony Siragusa, Will Demps, and Orlando Brown (the second time) are some of the team's top signings.

Newsome likes to do things in a routine, in a plan, with a certain eye to building a football team. And it's worked.

"This first thing is, you have to have a plan," Newsome said. "Then there have to be some results from [the plan]. People want to see that you're heading in the direction of winning. The salary cap doesn't allow you to be patient. There no longer can be anything such as a five-year plan."

Newsome's plan began when he retired after the 1990 season. His success as a tight end was well documented, as he made the NFL Hall of Fame plus three other Halls of Fame. He played 13 years with the Cleveland Browns as one of the game's best tight ends. Modell then hired him as a special assignment scout to begin his front office career.

Newsome later became the team's director of pro personnel (1994) after helping with some of the offensive coaching duties. Despite moving up in the front office, Newsome's low-key personality proved helpful. After signing Sharpe and then watching the former Bronco break his own record for catches by a tight end, Newsome congratulated and joked with him on the field.

In addition, Newsome was one of the people in charge of the Ravens' salary cap-induced roster change—when the team had to get rid of many players following the 2001 season and try to come up with a good draft and low-key free-agent signings. The Ravens were in the playoff fight heading into the final few games of 2002 despite fielding the youngest team in NFL history. The turnaround became even more complete in 2003, when the Ravens again relied on a good draft and, despite fielding a very young squad, won the AFC North. Newsome had a huge hand in all of the moves that made the Ravens a strong team.

The New Man in Charge

Many owners in professional sports have become like Broadway stars in recent years. They blow into town, make a million changes and try to take charge of something they know little about (see: Dan Snyder, Redskins) and just want to be "The Man."

But that didn't happen when Steve Bisciotti joined the team as its minority owner in 2000. Bisciotti, a lifelong Baltimore-area resident, purchased 49 percent of the team for $275 million with an option to buy the whole team in 2004. However, once Bisciotti joined the team, he did something different—he faded into the background.

Bisciotti let Modell have his final four years at the helm and stayed out of the spotlight. He was involved with the team in different ways but kept a low profile. Bisciotti said that he wanted to be able to learn how things worked from Modell.

"In many ways, Art is the NFL," Bisciotti said last summer. "I'd be short-sighted not to take advantage of his expertise."

Bisciotti founded Aerotek in 1983, which eventually became one of the world's top technical staffing firms. It's now known as Allegis Group and helped make Bisciotti a major success and helped set him up to purchase the Ravens.

It's doubtful that Bisciotti will come in and make major changes to a team that's been successful for so long. David Modell, the team's president and chief operating officer, already confirmed that he won't be back, and *The Baltimore Sun* reported in early February that Bisciotti was going to be bringing in Richard Cass, a Washington attorney, to be an executive who'd likely take most of Modell's duties.

The Beginning

The Cleveland Browns had been part of that city's heart for a very long time. They sold out games, had the infamous Dawg Pound, and boasted some of the most emotional fans in the National Football League.

But as the mid-'90s neared, team owner Art Modell faced some problems. He bought the team for the princely sum of $4 million in 1961 and was known as one of the NFL's most powerful owners. He was the NFL's broadcast chairman for 31 years, a driving force behind the start of ABC's *Monday Night Football.*

However, the Browns were having problems during the 1995 season. The team's home, Municipal Stadium, was long past its better days and an old war horse that caused numerous financial problems. Modell repeatedly talked with Cleveland politicians about building him a new stadium.

However, Modell simply could not get a new building built. The Indians got a plush new stadium, where they were selling out on a regular basis with one of the best young teams in Major League Baseball. The Rock and Roll Hall of Fame was built and attracted tons of visitors, and even the lowly Cleveland Cavaliers got a new basketball building, but still no stadium for Modell's Browns.

Other projects were being worked on, but Modell couldn't get his stadium. He couldn't seem to make any progress with the Ohio politicians and quietly began talking with people from Maryland. An article in *The Canton Repository*, talking about Modell last September, said that minority partner Al Lerner basically told Modell his options were simple—since you're not getting a stadium, sell the team or move it.

Modell didn't want to sell the team and cut a deal to move the team to Baltimore for the 1996 season. The move hit Cleveland like a bombshell. Modell looked grim at the initial press conference announcing the move in Baltimore in November, 1995.

Cleveland fans went nuts when they heard the news. Modell felt he had no choice, and the situation at that time still frustrates him over eight years later. He hasn't been back to Cleveland to see a game since the move.

"I could not go bankrupt," Modell said. "We built up so much debt in that old stadium. I had to do something to salvage my franchise and my family. I was not trying to hurt them. I love those people in Cleveland, but not the politicians and some leaders in the business community."

Modell felt he did all he could to avoid the move, but the politicians weren't able to help him in the right way.

"They [the politicians] lied to me," Modell said. "They sold me out. They took it for granted that Art Modell would never move the team. I have some regrets about...moving. I'm sorry I hurt people in the process. The fans there supported us very well."

Modell tried hard to smooth things over. He left the team's name and colors there—something Colts owner Robert Irsay didn't do when moving that team from Baltimore in March 1984. Interestingly, when Cleveland got an expansion franchise just three years later, the team got a new stadium very quickly.

So Modell set his sights on making Baltimore a great home for his football team. The going was tough at first. Moving an entire business along with people who work for you is expensive and tough in many ways.

The move wasn't officially approved by the NFL until February of 1996. That didn't leave much time for the team to get set up in Baltimore, but they were ready for the first season although some said later it was tough moving to another city.

Things moved a bit slowly at first. There was never anyone who said they didn't want the team, but many felt that because the team had come from another city—and Baltimore lost a team that way—it didn't feel like it was "our" team at first.

In addition, it didn't help that the Orioles were in the midst of making the playoffs for two straight years (1996-1997) and repeatedly drawing huge crowds to their baseball stadium, one of the best in the country.

I remember talking with Kevin Byrne, the team's vice president and head of community relations, during one of the early training camp practices in the summer of 1996, the team's first year here. It was a quiet day, and Byrne surprised me with a question.

"Hey, Jeff, how long do you think it will take before the city takes to the team?" Byrne asked.

"When they make the playoffs," I said, with a laugh.

The Colts memories were still too vivid and the team was still playing in the Colts' old house. But Modell did a lot of things that Irsay never did—he made himself available to the public, was constantly seen around town, talked endlessly to the media and set up an organization that answered to the community. That's a big reason the team and the community bonded so well.

Matte's Musings on Modell and the Move to Baltimore

"It was interesting. Prior to [the team's move], Memorial Stadium was in terrible condition. When we started the Stallions, the CFL team, I was a part owner and basically a sales-marketing kind of guy, and I got done all the things we needed to get done. We had problems with the water, we had problems with the sewage, we had pipes that were leaking all over the fans down there. The stadium was really in disarray. It was terrible. It took us two years to fix it up, and I got a couple of million dollars out of the state and the Stadium Authority. We had some help from state senator Tom Bromwell and some of the people down there who really wanted to get football back here.

"We also thought it was going to be an opportunity, if we fixed the stadium up, that it would enhance our chances of getting an NFL team. I think that's one of the things that helped. We were drawing probably 25,000 or 30,000 people a game to the Stallions, which is really good. It was a stepping stone for Modell to leave Cleveland. The problem with Modell was the politicians up there jerked him around. I mean they really jerked him around. They built a brand-new baseball stadium. They built a rock and roll hall of fame, they built a basketball thing, and Art was putting all of his own personal money into the renovation of that old stadium down there, which was antiquated when he took it over. And he was trying to make it because the Browns—to me, being a Cleveland kid—they were the most important thing in the world as far as I was concerned. When Modell came into the NFL the same year I did in 1961, he took over the Cleveland Browns from Paul Brown. He immediately got involved with the community up there. He really put a lot back into the community. He felt he was part of it, and with his wit and cynicism, people just loved him. He was just a hit with them, and when he married Pat, she just added more class to what he already was and they did a lot of work for the Cleveland Clinic up there and they did a lot of stuff like that.

"But what happened is that he overextended himself. His operating budget was just too high, and I don't know what the heck happened, but he was in a position where he really had to move. He didn't get that extra money from things like skyboxes. He needed that operating capital to be able to keep the franchise afloat. What he did do, and showed class doing it, was that he left that town, but he left all the tradition, all the names, all the records and everything with Cleveland, not like our good friend Mr. Irsay, who was a total jerk here in Baltimore when he moved the Colts. He had no class at all as far as I was concerned. With the Browns, it was a quiet thing. It did leak out at the end that it was working out, but we had a great crew there that was really working on it. It was behind the scenes. John Moag, the governor [Parris Glendening] and [former governor] William Donald Schaefer did a great job.

"There was a committee. Ernie Accorsi, now the Giants' GM, was part of that committee. In fact, my wife worked for Ernie for a while and was helping to bring the team back. We had a couple of preseason games, and we sold it out. We just sold it out. We had a great turnout because we wanted the NFL, we deserved to have the NFL back here. And I think that Art Modell thought that Baltimore pretty well got screwed when

Irsay left town. He said, 'Here's a town that has a great tradition in football, and I think I can make it work,' and he has. But that whole fan base up there wanted to kill him.

"He has not gone back to Cleveland because of death threats, and they blew it so far out of proportion to what was happening. They don't understand the business economics of what was happening with him. I don't think he made a mistake. How many times can you knock on the door and say, hey, I need a new stadium. Nobody helped him. They thought he was making so much money out of football that he didn't need any help. I'll tell you one thing—you have to have the community behind you. You have to have the state behind you and the Stadium Authority behind you like we have here. They did a great job. And let me tell you something, he would have been dumb if he wouldn't have taken this deal. It was a sweetheart deal. It was the best deal that has been out there, on the table for anybody, and he still had to put money into it later.

"He saw what was going to happen here. He saw the fan base growing. I think they've sold out just about every game since they've been here. I go back to when Irsay was here. The 12 years I played here, we had a sellout every game. That's true football. That's true fans. That's what he saw. I called him up, and I even asked him for a job. I said I've been through it all and I can really help you if you want to. I don't know what happened there. I think he may have been sidetracked by some of the other front office people saying we don't want to be associated with the Baltimore Colts, we want our own identity. I understood that. I really did. The only thing that upset me about it was that the guys who played here wanted the NFL team back here, and we would give them 100 percent support and all of the alumni here has given him 100 percent support with it. Baltimore Colt players are sort of in oblivion because there's no place we can identify with. We're caught in the middle. First of all, we've had no communication with Bob Irsay or Jimmy Irsay or anybody. They dropped us like a hot potato. We said, 'Hey, listen, we're not Indianapolis Colts, we're Baltimore Colts. So all those records that we've attained here in Baltimore should stay here in Baltimore and Indianapolis guys who set new records should have their own. So please expunge our records from the Indianapolis Colts.' But when Art Modell first came here, the first book that came out had the Colts, all the statistics from the Colts, which I thought again had a lot of class and said hey, we know the tradition of football here in Baltimore. We know that the fans and players had a relationship that was like what we had when I was with the Cleveland Browns. I think he saw that kind of franchise here. And then he brings in some great people with him. He brings in Ozzie Newsome here and some guys like Phil Savage and he wanted a coach initially to come in like Ted Marchibroda who was a transition coach. He was with the Colts here for a while and had just done a good job with Indianapolis and then came here to the Ravens."

One for the Owner

The Ravens knew that 2003 was Modell's final season as the team's owner. That's why many people associated with the team wanted him to go out with something special.

"I'd do anything in my power to end up in Houston [at the Super Bowl] on his last ride," Ray Lewis said.

Not many people gave the Ravens a chance to do that, however, as a very young team led by a rookie quarterback doesn't often impress a lot of folks. The rookie quarterback then went down midway through the season and was replaced by another inexperienced starter.

Modell wanted to have a special season also, but he remained very low-key about it. He gave the requisite interviews, said all the right things in a low-key manner, but everyone knew he would have been thrilled with another title.

Still, he was very happy to see the Ravens win their first division title with a 10-6 record, beating out the surprising Cincinnati Bengals by two games.

But Modell truly didn't want a huge amount of attention focused on him during his final year. He just wanted to do his normal things, sit in the ever-present golf cart and watch practice, talk to the players, coaches and reporters and enjoy his team.

"I don't want any fuss made about me or hoopla," Modell said. "I want us to have a great season, and then I want to walk away quietly. I'm proud of my career."

Art Modell addressing his team in the locker room. (Photo by Phil Hoffmann)

Why Not the Hall?

Still, the final missing piece to the Modell puzzle is the Hall of Fame. The move from Cleveland angered many, especially in that city's media, who repeatedly take shots at him, even eight years later.

But many who care for and respect Modell were hoping that he'd get the nomination and be voted in during this, his final season. It didn't happen, though, the only real sour taste to a very sweet year.

Modell, however, had said several times that it would be nice if the honor came his way but there's not much he can do about it.

"It would be nice to get into the Hall, but I have no control over the process," Modell said.

Several journalists wrote pieces talking about how much Modell meant to the NFL during his long 43-year association with the league. Modell's work that helped the television deals grow to what they are today—bringing in so much revenue for the league—have truly been crucial to the league's success and growth as one of the country's most prominent sports leagues.

Most people felt that this alone would finally be enough to get him the nomination and eventual vote to the Hall.

"Art changed the game, really revolutionized it," said Baltimore kicker Matt Stover. "He and Pete Rozelle had the foresight to see what the NFL could become. They spearheaded the expansion of the league. Art helped make a very popular game marketable and profitable without sacrificing his integrity."

Baltimore general manager Ozzie Newsome said the same thing.

"He's a great contributor to this league," Newsome said. "Art is a man who has always put the NFL and his team first. He has sacrificed for this team. He has a lot of passion for football."

Many in the NFL believe that Modell should have a shot at the Hall of Fame simply because of what he's done over nearly four and a half decades.

"I believe that in the near future his entire record should be recognized as entitling him to be in the Hall of Fame in Canton," NFL commissioner Paul Tagliabue said. "Art Modell is a legend of our game and one of life's unforgettable characters for all of us who have been fortunate to know him."

The question is, now that Modell won't be an active participant in the league, will it lessen his chances of making the Hall of Fame? Everyone will just have to wait and see.

The Quieter Modell

David Modell wasn't quite as well known as his father, but he had a quiet role in many things that the Ravens accomplished since moving to Baltimore in 1996.

He worked with the team while it was in Cleveland and eventually worked his way up and served as team president and chief operating officer (when the team moved to Baltimore) and did a large number of behind-the-scenes things that many fans don't realize. Modell was the person who led the effort to bring Billick to Baltimore as head coach, the move to the new stadium in 1998 and getting over 100,000 people to touch the Super Bowl trophy after the team won the championship in 2000.

But he was scheduled to exit quietly after Bisciotti took over the team in the spring of 2004. Bisciotti was bringing in Richard Cass to take over most of what Modell did and handled.

Modell didn't get quite as much media attention as his father but still found his way around town plenty and got on television and radio enough to be known. Although his father was the better known of the Modell men, most associated with the franchise admit the younger Modell certainly did his part.

A Real TV Winner

Reality television has become hot the past few seasons, and ABC's *The Bachelorette* is one of the shows that many people took an interest in.

Why is this in a book about the Ravens? The reason—when Trista surprised the TV viewing audience and picked Ryan in the show's finale, it had a real connection with the Ravens.

Ryan is Ryan Sutter, who was Baltimore's fifth-round pick in the 1998 NFL draft. Sutter played safety at Colorado and was cut late in the 1998 training camp. He then signed with the Carolina Panthers a few days later and spent much of that season on the practice squad.

Sutter finally made the active roster on November 28, 1998, but got put on injured reserve a week later. He then signed with Seattle the following summer, but was cut and hasn't made it back to the NFL since.

But Savage and the Ravens had some comments on Sutter's victory. "We're the only team that can boast taking Jonathan Ogden and Ray Lewis with our first-ever selections and drafting the winner of *The Bachelorette*," said Savage.

How to Be a TV Star

HBO Sports and NFL Films called it the first sports-based reality series. The reason: they were allowed to film things and get access that no one had ever really had before.

In the series titled *Hard Knocks: Training Camp with the Baltimore Ravens*, viewers saw six one-hour episodes that aired literally the week they were filmed as the team made its way through training camp.

Viewers saw Billick addressing the team, talking to the coaches about whom to cut and deciding the moves to make. They also saw him talking quietly to the players while actually cutting them from the active roster and making suggestions about what they could do with their football lives.

"I think it's pretty cool," then-defensive tackle Tony Siragusa said during the second week of filming. "I think people don't really understand what players go through when they come and report to camp."

The cameras followed Siragusa and tight end Shannon Sharpe all over the place and gave people a glance at the interesting sense of humor the two players have. Viewers saw Siragusa give rookie first-round pick Todd Heap some good-natured—and rather loud—ribbing in the team's dining room about the contract the tight end had signed as the team's top draft pick.

They saw Sharpe's loud and nearly painful reaction to Heap's attempts at singing the Arizona State fight song. Sharpe jumped up, squealed, and fell over backwards. But he was laughing the whole time, so it was easy to see that this was a joke.

"It isn't a big change," Sharpe said. "Early on, you find yourself looking to see if they're around, but after a while you've just got to be yourself. You've just got to say, 'Okay, if the cameras weren't here, this is what I would have said, this is what I would have done, this is what I would have eaten.' I'm going to do what I normally do."

Siragusa said that having the cameras follow him would go a long way towards answering the sometimes annoying questions they get about life in training camp.

"People ask me, 'Do you stay at home? Where do you stay? What do you do? Do you guys play golf a lot?'" Siragusa said. "I get the craziest questions. Now all I have to do is say, 'Turn on HBO and check it out, and you'll see what we do.'"

Baltimore coach Brian Billick said that it gave football fans a true look at life in an NFL training camp.

"It's a classy piece, and I think NFL Films is doing a hell of a job," Billick said during the second week. "I think people are going to get a feel for the personality of some of the guys we have. There are some intriguing stories here."

Safety Rod Woodson said that the Ravens had a lot of unusual stories because they were an unusual team. At that time, they were the defending Super Bowl champions, and everyone knew they were a colorful team.

Billick often just rolled his eyes when asked about the nature of his team. That's why Woodson laughed when asked how much fun the Ravens enjoyed during camp.

"We have fun here," he said. "We have a lot of clowns on this team, a lot of colorful people on this football team who are very loose. Each locker room has its own colorful individuals, but we have a lot, a whole lot...and some are bigger than others."

Todd TV

Heap actually got more television attention than most of the other Ravens before he played a down with the team.

The NFL Films/HBO crews have paid him lots of notice as part of the *Hard Knocks* series. But Heap handled all of the attention—and it came on a personal basis—very smoothly for a rookie coming to a team that had just won the Super Bowl.

After being filmed for several days in several ways, Heap simply smiled when asked if he'd learned anything.

"I still don't look good on TV," he said with a laugh. "That's all I've learned so far."

The extra attention didn't bother Heap very much. He did a smooth job of blocking out everything and simply concentrating on his work on the field.

TV star Todd Heap is ready for his close-up. (Photo by Mitchell Layton)

The bottom line—being filmed constantly wasn't a distraction.

"I just kind of do the same things I've always done," he said. "I don't really think about it too much. The films and the camera—that's the last thing on your mind out there."

The crews got a true virtual all-access pass from the Ravens, which opened the door to Heap's personal life in a way that would have bothered many players, not just rookies.

At the beginning, the series showed his wedding to Ashley Rohner, their arrival in Baltimore a little later, and the groom carrying his new bride over the threshold. In addition, viewers got to see the Heaps' new Baltimore home and their first attempts at decorating during some rare free time.

The cameras also showed Heap as he tried to carefully fit in with his new teammates after their Super Bowl-winning season. He received plenty of lessons from Sharpe in addition to the traditional hazing, which Heap handled with perfect style.

"I'm surprised at how nice of a guy and how genuine he is," veteran running back Obafemi Ayanbadejo said during the first few days of camp. "He smiles and laughs things off. There's guys who've gone through worse than he has, but he's doing good and handling it well."

The first two shows let viewers see the things that rookies like Heap had to go through to become part of NFL life. The Ravens' veterans made Heap sing his Arizona State fight song in the team dining room and forced him to carry Sharpe's shoulder pads—in addition to his own—to the locker room after daily practices.

Heap liked what he saw in the episodes but did hope he looked a bit more stylish when on film in the future.

"I think it turned out well," he said. "NFL Films [did] a great job. I think our team's going to have fun with it."

Why T.O. Flew the Coop Before He Landed in the Nest, The Jamal Indictment, Free Agent Signings and Other Off-Season Things

Terrell Owens and Jamal Lewis were the two biggest stories in the first part of the 2004 off season, but the Ravens also had some good things happen during the winter.

The Ravens re-signed some key players—center Mike Flynn, offensive tackle Orlando Brown, defensive lineman/linebacker/special teams ace Adalius Thomas and back-up quarterback Anthony Wright, all of whom will help the team defend its AFC North title.

But Lewis and Owens do bring up some questions. The Ravens looked sharp by pulling off the deal with San Francisco that appeared to bring Owens to town for just a second-round draft pick.

Owens, however, began complaining pretty quickly about the trade and made it very clear that he wasn't thrilled about coming to Baltimore. He wanted to go to Philadelphia, thought he had a deal with the Eagles in place to be traded there, and thought the 49ers were trying to put the screws to him one final time.

As time went on, however, Owens began complaining louder and louder. He eventually filed a grievance with the NFL Players Association against the trade, asking to be declared a free agent. Owens was generally believed to have little chance at overturning the deal, but his legal team apparently presented a strong case to an arbitrator, and the Ravens stepped back and agreed to a three-team trade that sent the receiver to the Eagles while giving the Ravens draft choices.

The Ravens really appeared to get the raw end of the deal. They didn't re-sign wide receiver Marcus Robinson, who went to Minnesota while the Owens situation remained in limbo, and got basically just one draft pick for a Pro Bowl wide receiver.

Interestingly, Baltimore meets Philadelphia twice in 2004—once in the preseason and again in the regular season—both times on the road.

The Jamal Lewis situation also remained in limbo in the spring after the Pro Bowl. Lewis was indicted in February on federal drug charges as he was accused of helping a childhood friend buy cocaine. Lewis surrendered to officials in Atlanta, hired the same lawyer that teammate Ray Lewis used—Ed Garland—and began to fight the charges.

As of April, Jamal Lewis's situation remained unclear, although speculation was growing that a trial—if necessary—wouldn't take place until after the 2004 season ended.

Lewis and Garland vehemently denied the charges from the start and repeatedly expressed confidence that the running back would be cleared.

Stay tuned.

Chapter 2

MOVING TO
BALTIMORE:
RECONNECTING FOOTBALL
WITH THE COMMUNITY

Welcome Home, Mr. Irsay

The way that the Baltimore Colts left the city in March of 1984, sneaking out late at night and not telling anyone what was going on, left a very bad taste in the mouths of local sports fans for a very long time.

It's doubtful that Colts fans would have liked their departure in any form, but the way that owner Robert Irsay had behaved since he purchased the team in 1972 made him rather unpopular in the city—and the way he left just added to that.

So when the Colts came back to Baltimore for the first time to play the Ravens on November 29, 1998, there clearly was some real emotion in the city. That emotion was only intensified by the way the Ravens rallied from a big first-half deficit for a 38-31 victory.

Indianapolis jumped out to a big early lead that day, but the Ravens roared back to win. That got the fans rather excited—

especially the ones sitting in front of the press box when they realized who was sitting there.

Late in the first half, several fans recognized that Jimmy Irsay was sitting in the second row of the press box near the 40-yard line. He's been running the franchise for several years and is a much quieter personality than his late father.

But the Ravens fans didn't really care about that on this day. It's likely that this was the first time Baltimore faithful had seen an Irsay in town since that fateful night when the team left. And he didn't get the greatest reception.

First, a few began pointing towards Irsay and laughing. The numbers slowly began to grow as the Ravens began to come back. Some fans then started pounding on the glass—the press box is enclosed—and screaming a sampling of the seven words you can't say on television.

They kept giving Irsay the finger, cursing at him and laughing. It got worse as the game went on, but he never said a word or reacted to it, sitting there stone-faced as his Colts blew a big lead. Truth be told, that took some class.

The First Coach

The Ravens hired former Baltimore Colts head coach Ted Marchibroda as their first coach soon after coming to town. Marchibroda was one of the more popular coaches in Baltimore history because he took over a losing team in 1975 and turned them around to win the AFC Eastern Division three straight years.

In addition, Marchibroda became a bit of a cult hero for a while in Baltimore because he told off Irsay and walked away. The team went 10-4 and won the AFC East in the coach's first year in 1975—after going 2-12 the previous year—and then struggled in the preseason the next year.

Irsay stumbled into the dressing room after one of the preseason losses, reportedly somewhat on the drunk side, and made some silly remarks. Marchibroda then quit, but eventually came back about a day later when the players rose up in his defense. Baltimore fans loved him for that and enjoyed it even more when he was hired to coach the Ravens.

Interestingly enough, Marchibroda came to the Ravens after a second stint with the Colts in Indianapolis (1992-1995). He didn't like how he was treated after the Colts surprisingly made the AFC title game in his final year, and he resigned. The Ravens hired him soon afterward.

The media loved Marchibroda because he was a soft-spoken, nice guy who always seemed happy. He also seemed to know everyone. But his tenure with the Ravens was doomed almost from the start.

The team was in a state of transition during the 1996 season, as many were still adjusting to living in a new city and setting up their lives in a new place. The Ravens also had very little in the way of defense and finished just 4-12 the first year.

Marchibroda was optimistic coming into the second year as quarterback Vinny Testaverde came in off a Pro Bowl season with a young defense that had another year's experience. The team started 3-1 and the town got excited—but the Ravens faded badly after that and finished 6-9-1.

Year three brought more of the same as new quarterback Jim Harbaugh played well enough while battling through injuries, and the Ravens never got going and finished 6-10. There were questions about how well Marchibroda related to the younger generation of players and whether they tuned him out a bit as the losses mounted—he was only 16-31-1 over three seasons.

The team fired him right after the 1998 season, a painful move for team management, as they genuinely liked him as a person.

The Band That Would Not Stop Playing

When the Colts left town, the team's marching band was put into a state of flux. They wanted to keep playing, but there was no team.

However, this group had been in this situation before.

The Baltimore Colts band was formed in 1947 while the team played in the All-America Conference. But the team folded after the 1950 season. The band kept playing, however, during 1951 and 1952, helping the NFL to remember Baltimore.

The Dallas Texans moved to Baltimore in 1953 and became the Colts. The marching band joined with the team and its popularity grew throughout the years in the city and the league.

The band still wanted to keep going after the Colts left town. So they decided to stay active, hoping that pro football would find its way back to town at some point.

"It was determination," said John Ziemann, who served as percussion instructor and public relations director when the Colts left town. "[Irsay] took the heart of the community,

The band performs at the last professional game at Memorial Stadium. (Photo courtesy of John Ziemann)

packed it up in trucks and put it away. But the sun came up the next day and nobody died."

Ziemann said that members of the band decided that they would not let Irsay's move silence them. They'd keep playing to make the NFL remember Baltimore.

"I pledged, along with the members of the band, that we'd continue the band, keep the spirit up," Ziemann said. "We'd go around the nation, perform at other NFL games, showing the spirit and enthusiasm for professional football in Baltimore and perform on the home front in keeping the spirit and enthusiasm up."

So the band just kept playing. The Colts' fight song drew standing ovations when the band played in Baltimore long after the team left town; it still gives some chills even today. The band kept showing up at NFL games all over the country and playing.

But the band helped in other ways. In the late '80s, then governor William Donald Schaefer was battling the Maryland legislature to try to get the money needed for a new stadium to house a possible new NFL team.

The problem—Schaefer seemed to be losing ground and losing his fight. If the state couldn't build another stadium, then the likelihood of luring another team back to Baltimore was very slim.

Ziemann said that Schaefer was told on a Friday that he didn't have even one civic group that would stand up for him and support his bid. That's when the band took over.

The following Monday, the band showed up on the statehouse steps in Annapolis playing the Colts fight song. The bill passed later that week, and the football and baseball stadiums received the funds.

"Schaefer said that's the night that turned the tide," Ziemann said. "It stirred up the area's civic pride."

The band kept playing during the 12 football seasons when Baltimore didn't have any teams. During that time, about 175 people stayed with the band and kept playing. That's why things got even better when the Modells brought the Browns to town for the 1996 seasons.

The Ravens and the band agreed that it should keep the name "Colts Marching Band" for the team's first two years in town because that would let it mark a 50-year anniversary. In addition, the Ravens were set to play in Memorial Stadium, which was the Colts' home for their stay in Baltimore.

The Ravens moved into their new stadium in 1998, and the band took on the name "Baltimore's Marching Ravens" after that and began to grow in a huge way. The band now has about 400 members and continues to be known as one of the NFL's most popular groups.

They practice on a regular basis for most of the year and show up at a number of big-name events, including the 2001 inauguration of President George W. Bush. But they were truly the group that wouldn't let the football fire die in Baltimore. Ziemann was a driving force behind this, along with his wife, Charlene, who was a Colts cheerleader and later a flag line instructor.

This group had a passion for Baltimore football. They truly helped get a team back to town. Simply put, the band played on.

"We just were not going to stop playing," Ziemann said.

Matte's Musings on the Band

"The band is the one that, to me, was the belt that held the pants up to keep the drive alive to get football back here in Baltimore. John Ziemann did an unbelievable job with it. I mean, the people who participated in the band are from every walk of life. If you take a look, there's some young kids out there, there's some old dogs out there. You take a look at the flag corps. Yes, these are fans. They're big fans. I can still remember the Colts fight song that we had here. Did we hear it? Oh, God, yes we heard it. You bet we did. I can still remember days when Loudy Loudenslager, our number one fan, would be at the airport when we left with his little 45. Somebody would always get his attention, and I'd sneak behind him and unplug it. And we'd come home at three or four in the morning, he was always there. He was always there for us, and the fight song was always there. We'd always unplug it then, too. All through those years, that band stayed together, they played when we had the Baltimore Stallions. I had the band out there playing. I told them, you come on out, you've got a home here any time you want it. Ziemann kept that group together and traveled to other NFL cities, played for them. They were still known as the Baltimore Colts Marching Band. It was certainly unique. I think it's probably the most unique band that there is in the NFL. It's not a small band. It's a pretty damn big band. They get out there and he utilizes it. He works those people. They've got to come and practice because if you don't practice, you don't play. He's kept the unity and the tradition of football here in Baltimore alive when it was dead."

The Uniforms

The Colts had uniforms that everyone in Baltimore recognized during their three-decade stay in town. Everyone loved the blue jerseys with white pants. Fans also loved the helmet with the ever-present horseshoe.

The jerseys and the horseshoe showed up all around town in a number of ways. The horseshoe—staying with the tradition of pointing up because if it was down, the luck would run out—was on T-shirts, hats, and just about anything else.

That's why so many people were curious to see what the Ravens would wear, especially at home. The Modells left the Browns' name and colors in Cleveland, so they came up with purple and white to be the main colors.

The team first wore purple jerseys with black pants at home – something they unveiled at a fashion show downtown in June of 1996. The helmets also had a shield with the letter "B" in the middle.

The purple colors caught on quickly. Purple T-shirts, sweatshirts, jackets, jerseys, hats and many other things began showing up all over Baltimore. The team changed its home outfits in year two, going to white pants, and later changed its helmet design due to legal wranglings, switching to a bird with a "B" in it.

But no matter what it was, if it was the Ravens, it was all over the place in Baltimore.

Goodbye, Memorial Stadium

Memorial Stadium was once the most feared stadium in the National Football League. During the glory days of the Baltimore Colts, the building was nicknamed "The World's Largest Outdoor Insane Asylum" by Chicago sportswriter Cooper Rollow, who was impressed by the noise and what a real advantage it became.

The Ravens had to play there in the franchise's first two years in Baltimore as the new stadium was being built a few minutes away. The old stadium wasn't quite as much of an advantage for the Ravens; the team won only 10 games during the first two years, but Baltimore residents were thrilled to see the old building up and moving again.

The stadium was obviously past its time—it was nearly 45 years old by the time the Ravens played their last game there in

December of 1997—and other teams were making millions off private suites in new buildings that Baltimore couldn't have yet. But there weren't too many complaints about the team playing there.

However, it was probably something that kept the Ravens from earning a stronger identity with the city in the early days. Memorial Stadium was the Colts' house—and later the home of the Canadian Football League entry called the Stallions for two years—and the Ravens were in a bit of an unusual position.

But the team handled it well and brought back many old Colts to say goodbye at the stadium's final game in December, 1997. Players like Tom Matte, Johnny Unitas, Lenny Moore and all kinds of big names returned for an emotional afternoon as the Ravens edged Tennessee, 21-19.

There was a post game ceremony with many of the old Colts on the field, wearing their trademark home blue jerseys, and posing for hundreds of pictures. But while the memories were great, one thing was for certain. It was time to move.

The New House

The Ravens moved into their new stadium in 1998, and the building was popular from the start. Fans loved the great site lines—you were only several yards away from the field in the first row of seats—and sellouts were regular.

The fans quickly took to the new stadium. They grew nearly as loud as Memorial Stadium crowds and, as the team became a winning club, made life difficult for the visiting teams. The stadium had two huge video boards that the team used to fire up the fans and a huge press box that most reporters enjoyed.

The only question was its name. In this era of marriage between the corporate world and sports, the Ravens couldn't find a partner right away, and the stadium didn't have a name for the first year. Most people called it some form of The Stadium at Camden Yards.

But 1999 brought a new name for the stadium. PSINet Inc., the first and largest independent commercial internet service provider, reached a 20-year agreement to call the new building PSINet Stadium.

That changed, however, when the business faded, and the stadium lost its name before the 2002 season. Most people called it Ravens Stadium for that year. But things changed in May 2003. The Ravens and M&T Bank entered into a long-term deal—specifically, a 15-year, $75 million agreement that included naming rights to the Ravens' home field at Camden Yards, which became "M&T Bank Stadium," as well as several important community-focused programs that would be jointly administered.

"This is a win-win-win situation," said Art Modell when the agreement was announced. "The Ravens win, because we stay competitive with other NFL teams in our quest for another Super Bowl championship; M&T Bank wins, because they become instantly established in the hearts and minds of our fans; and the Baltimore region wins, because of our shared commitment to this great community."

The Petition

Petitions don't often have too much value in the world of sports. When fans are upset about something or have an opinion, they'll usually talk to fellow sports fans, call a radio talk show or simply get angry.

But when the Ravens were still looking for a name for their stadium during the 2002 season, they found themselves facing an interesting proposition. Longtime Baltimore legend Johnny

Unitas died on September 11, 2002, and fans quickly started a petition to get the anonymous stadium named in his honor.

And it wasn't just a few people who joined the drive. Nearly 58,000 people signed the petition, which drew loads of attention. But naming a stadium is now a multimillion-dollar business, so the proposition couldn't really be considered strongly. However, the Ravens honored Unitas by putting up a statue in front of the stadium and a large picture as part of plaza named after him.

Here's a look at the emotional petition that made its way around Baltimore.

To: Baltimore Ravens and Baltimore Stadium Authority

1. Johnny Unitas died on 9/11/2002, aged 69. We, the undersigned, recognize the following:

Football returned to Baltimore in 1996 with the arrival of the Baltimore Ravens. The Ravens played their first two seasons in Memorial Stadium, the same venue as the old Baltimore Colts. In 1998, the Ravens moved into what would eventually become PSINet stadium. In 2002, after the demise of PSINet (the company), the name was removed and the stadium is now commonly referred to as "Ravens Stadium."

In 2001, demolition of Memorial Stadium began. The front facade of Memorial Stadium had the following inscribed upon it: "Dedicated as a memorial to all who so valiantly fought in the world wars with eternal gratitude to those who made the supreme sacrifice to preserve equality and freedom throughout the world—time will not dim the glory of their deeds."

Although many tried to save the facade and its message, the letters were removed and the final part of the old Memorial Stadium was demolished. The citizens of Baltimore are being told that the letters and the original wordage of the memorial will be reconstructed in the area between Oriole Park and Ravens Stadium.

The late Johnny Unitas, Hall Of Fame (1979) quarterback for the Baltimore Colts, named "Greatest Player in the First 50 Years of Pro Football," named "Player of the Decade" for the 1960s, three-time NFL

MVP, who completed 290 touchdown passes, who passed for over 40,000 yards, who won three NFL championships and had 26 games with over 300 yards passing and is widely regarded as the greatest quarterback ever, should be recognized and honored in the following manner.

We request that the current Baltimore Ravens Football Stadium be permanently renamed: JOHNNY UNITAS MEMORIAL STADIUM.

It would give pride to the city of Baltimore, honor Mr. Unitas and his contribution to Baltimore in particular and football in general and continue the memorial to fallen heroes with the use of the original lettering somewhere in the grounds of the stadium.

It is the right thing to do. We ask that the Baltimore Stadium Authority and The Baltimore Ravens Organization consider our request.

Thank you.

Sincerely,
The Undersigned

Helping with the Community

Ravens ownership is committed to getting players to give back to the community off the field.

The Ravens have promoted a very strong network of players who work hard to raise a large amount of money for various organizations, charities and foundations.

Ray Lewis is one of the players who worked hard at raising money. Lewis held his second annual celebrity auction and bowling tournament last May, and the Ray Lewis Foundation raised an impressive $120,000. The foundation provides personal and financial assistance for disadvantaged and at-risk youth.

Ogden established the Jonathan Ogden Foundation, which helps students in city schools reach their full potential using athletics and education. The Ogden Club also gets tutors to work

Edwin Mulitalo, one of many Ravens active in the community.
(Photo by Mitchell Layton)

with Baltimore City high school students, and they then tutor
local elementary school students.

Jamal Lewis founded the "Another Love for One
Foundation" which tries to improve life for low-income individuals. Boulware sponsored 16 youth tackle teams in the

Baltimore City Department of Parks & Recreation in the fall of 2003. He also works as a spokesperson for the NFL Punt, Pass & Kick Tournament in Baltimore as well as the NFL Flag Football Festival in Baltimore County.

McAlister hosts an annual golf tournament in Tucson, Arizona, that helps raise money for the Boys & Girls Club.

Mulitalo is a big music fan and established "Big Ed's Band Foundation," which gave musical instruments to the city schools.

This is just a short list of the different ways Ravens players did things to connect with the community. It's something the Modells wanted and something that made the community happy.

"Here, the extraordinary must be commonplace," Modell said in his mission statement for the team.

Matte's Musings on the Community

"I don't think there will ever be a sports team again that had the relationship the Colt players had with the fans. We live in a different time. There's free agency. There's no stability as far as your team goes. There's a lot of changeover. Maybe three or four guys would come into your team in one year—max, maybe two—when I played with the Colts. You take a look at the wholesale changes that happened two years ago after they won the Super Bowl and they had to get the salary cap down.

"There's always going to be a few guys who are going to be an integral part of the community like the Ray Lewises and the Jonathan Ogdens. But there's always going to be a high changeover. When Irsay came along here, fans dropped off because of the ownership. Now since Modell's been here, I don't think we've ever had a game where we didn't have a sellout, even though we didn't have the best records in the world for a while.

We came out and were always competitive. There's a relation-ship, there's a different crowd that goes to games. There's a younger crowd, the 25-45 ages. If you take a look at the Colts as they grew, all the people grew with the Colts and it became an older crowd. They lived and died with us. I mean, they knew our children's names, they knew our birthdays, we got birthdays cards and cakes from fans. They'd write notes to you. We were such a part of the community.

"The Ravens are doing the same thing. I just spoke to the Ravens Nest recently. I sat there for two hours and told them stories. They were mesmerized. It was a young crowd, mostly under 45 years of age. It's a younger crowd now; they're into the game. They just love the Ravens, and it's a good thing. I see it continue to grow all the time. Will it ever get to the extent of what the Colts were? No, I don't think so. The Colt Corrals were in all the neighborhood bars. We'd do four of them in a week. We'd get 25 bucks for one of them and the rest we'd do for noth-ing. It was really a bonding between the fans and the players. Players in today's world don't want to do that. It's a different time. People still come up to me today and pull out a picture of them sitting on the school benches at our camp in Westminster. They'll say, I still have this picture in my wallet and you were so nice to the guys. That's the kind of thing that Modell has tried to do, and Bisciotti will continue to do it. I think he had a lot of respect for Modell, and he let Modell have his time and he did it the right way. You can't say enough about Steve and his family. He's been very, very successful and been very blessed. He's a hard worker. He wanted to get this team very badly. He paid $600 million for it and worked his buns off. He's still work-ing his buns off to make it happen. Do I think he's going to change anything? Why fix it if it's not broken?

"He may have some management people that he wants to come on in there to oversee. I think that [in] the infrastructure I see right now, I don't think there will be too many changes being made. Hopefully, the broadcasting stays the same. I think

Scott Garceau and I have done a pretty good job. We've been with the team since the beginning, and it's probably one of my most fun things I do in life. We'd like to keep doing it, and we'll see what happens. Scott and I have been working together from way back when the Baltimore Colts were in preseason games when Ernie Accorsi was here as the general manager. We were hired because we were friends of Ernie's. I think we did a good job, and I think we have been doing a good job. I think we're highly recognizable as a team, which is nice. I don't think there's anybody more knowledgeable than Scotty is in preparation for a game, in understanding the game itself. We laugh and giggle. We have fun all the time. We just have a great time. It's a nice little tight-knit group, and during the game we're laughing the whole time."

Chapter 3

BRIAN BILLICK AND HIS COACHES

The Coach

Brian Billick was not exactly a household name when the Ravens hired him shortly after the 1998 season ended. Billick came to the Ravens after putting together a Minnesota offense that spent 1998 setting an NFL mark for points scored in a season (556). During his five years as Minnesota's offensive coordinator, Billick's Vikings had their top three offensive seasons and five of the top 10 in franchise history.

Both the Ravens and Browns were very interested in Billick following Minnesota's tremendous offensive success, but the Ravens got their man. Billick was a different sort of coach than previous head man Ted Marchibroda.

The older Marchibroda was more of an old-school kind of guy. During camp, the Ravens sweated through two-a-days in pads and often worked in pads throughout the season. But even though Billick hadn't been an NFL head coach, he turned things around and set up a bit of a different schedule.

Billick worked at shortening training camp and making it easier for the players to get through—trying hard to stay away from the injuries. He wanted the team to be healthy and ready later in the season.

The Ravens began doing two-a-days in the camp but often went without pads in the day's second workout. The second practice was also shorter than the first, to take the strain off players.

Rod Woodson joked to Billick that the Baltimore camps were often "like Club Med" compared to other camps he'd been through. Billick also made in-season practices without pads later in the season to lower the risk of injuries. He also works extremely hard at teaching and motivating, something that players say was vital to the team's success during his five years on the job.

"I'm a teacher," Billick said. "I've been around great coaches—Tom Landry and Bill Walsh and LaVell Edwards and Denny Green and Doug Scovil—and they all had divergent personalities, but the commonality was that they were all excellent teachers."

Billick also has been very good at taking the positive points out of almost any situation. During the 2000 season, when the Ravens went five games without scoring a touchdown, Billick kept the team together and helped stop infighting.

Later in the season, when the team clinched its first playoff spot, Billick did something unusual. He gave out a schedule for the team—one that went all the way through the Super Bowl. The subtle message was that, hey, we're good enough to make it that far.

And they did. Billick's self-assured demeanor ticked off some others in the league and the national media. It's been that way ever since, but Billick's lone concern is getting his team best prepared to be a winner. The Ravens did that in 2003 despite

Brian Billick celebrates on the sidelines after a Ravens score. (Photo by Phil Hoffmann)

being a very young team that had some real problems in spots. Still, they won the division with a 10-6 record.

"I don't like to be No. 2 at anything," Billick said. "I say that tongue in cheek, [but] in this job, if you have success—and especially if you win a Super Bowl—at some point you're going to be accused of being arrogant."

Billick's been accused of being arrogant. And cocky. And too self-assured. And he doesn't care. He does whatever is necessary to make the Ravens ready to play each Sunday.

"Brian didn't get enough credit because maybe we weren't the 35- to 40-point scoring offense that he had in Minnesota," said Cincinnati coach Marvin Lewis, a former Baltimore defensive coordinator. "But we were an efficient offense that moved the football, that scored when we needed to. Even when we weren't scoring touchdowns, we weren't giving the other team the ball deep in our territory. As people ask me that question,

Brian Billick proudly displays the Lombardi Trophy. (Photo by Phil Hoffmann)

that has been my response, 'that maybe you are not giving that man enough credit for what he did.'"

Matte's Musings on Coach Billick

"My estimation is what he's done as far as being a success here is that he knows how to handle his players. He protects his players, he keeps them healthy for a season, he doesn't run them into the ground, he doesn't burn them out, and he respects their talents. He has no curfews. What other coach does that? When I played, we always had a curfew of 11 p.m. No road curfew at all for them. The players are treated as adults, and I think that's something that Billick does well.

"I think that Billick is a great motivator. I think he knows what buttons to push with which players. I think that was one of the keys to Don Shula's success is that he knew his players so well that he knows what button to push on them to make sure he'll get the maximum effort out of them. Shula was more of a disciplinarian, while Billick is more of a politician. What you want to hear Billick say, he says. He's a media star. He says things the right way. The key to it, to me, and I've talked to a lot of people about this, is that he really takes care of his players. He really does. As far as the offensive guru that he's supposed to be, well, it's the defense that's really stabilized things. I think that we'll be very competitive. If the Ravens can hold on to Chris McAlister and Adalius Thomas, I think we're going to have another great defensive ball club that will keep us in the games all the way. Jim Fassel will help improve the offense, and that should be a big plus.

"Billick gets ripped all the time with the national media. People think he has a big ego. He can go out on the motivational speech tour and probably make more money than 98 percent of the population because he is a great speaker. If you've ever listened to him speak to a business group or anything like that, you'll see the guy is a motivator. The guy knows what to say. He was in public relations when he got into the National Football League. He knows what the press wants to hear.

"But he also plays with them. He comes up with all kinds of little zingers at you. Even our radio show that I do, he'll even call in and give me a shot. I love it. I think it's great. I think it's fun. I sort of laugh at it because he is very intelligent. I think he's a very intelligent coach. I think he knows how to be able to manipulate the media a little bit. And I think the media gets a little bit upset, and I think that's what they get upset about. I have a chance to sit down and talk with Billick. Scott Garceau and I do a lot of interviews prior to the game. He charts everything out. He looks at how we can take advantage of it and all that stuff. Execution, however, is the name of the game. Coaches coach, but players play. Coaches have got to make decisions and then they have to live with those decisions."

Game Balls

Billick gives out game balls in an interesting way. He does it to congratulate, call attention, and remind people of things.

One of the more interesting instances involving game balls came after Baltimore's wild 44-41 overtime victory over Seattle in 2003.

The Ravens had played poorly and were trailing by 17 before new starting quarterback Anthony Wright sparked a fourth-quarter rally to tie the game and send it to overtime. Wright had barely played in his five NFL seasons, throwing a grand total of 151 passes before he took over following Kyle Boller's injury and backup Chris Redman's shaky performance in relief.

Orlando Brown can be counted on for solid play on the offensive line. Once, however, he received a game ball for his work on defense. (Photo by Mitchell Layton)

But despite the pressure of finally getting a chance to play, Wright had even more on his mind. His wife, Nicole, was ready to be induced into labor for the birth of their daughter Trinity. The overtime game took about four hours because of an extra period and ended around 5 p.m.

Wright went to the hospital afterward to be with his wife, who was induced around 8 p.m. She had the baby a few days later. So what did Billick do? He gave the game ball to Wright.

Nicole, that is.

"She gets it for waiting until 8 [to be induced]," Billick said. "As I told the players in there, you have no concept. I don't want to hear about pain. I don't want to hear about 'I'm hurt,' because you have no concept of it. My second daughter was induced, and that's an interesting experience."

The other game ball that day went to Orlando Brown. The Ravens had practiced putting the mammoth 350-pound offensive lineman on defense for short-yardage situations. They used Brown as a type of nose tackle who helped stop Seattle on fourth down late in regulation. That gave the Ravens the ball back and set up a quick drive to tie the game.

Billick then gave the defensive game ball to Brown.

"You look at the picture in [the paper], it's interesting where [Seattle quarterback] Hasselbeck is, because he couldn't go there," Billick said. "Because all 750 pounds of Orlando was right there over the nose, twice. It is kind of what it's about: a player from the opposite side of the ball. We need him for a specific purpose. We practiced it, and he goes in and does his job phenomenally."

Billick did something similar a few weeks later when the Ravens blanked Cleveland, 35-0, in a key late-season game. He wanted to show the team the importance of basic teamwork afterward and give out no game balls since the offense, defense and special teams all helped. But the defense reminded him of the team's tradition of giving out balls to the entire defense after a shutout.

And so he did just that.

The Words You Can't Say to the Media

Billick has long been known as, well, outspoken on many subjects. This is a coach who will tell you what he feels when he feels it.

But he gained national attention after a little outburst following Baltimore's 26-6 win over Denver. Billick was infuriated when the officials wouldn't rule his way on two coach's challenges involving the Ravens.

Billick came into the game upset about a few things that happened with instant replay during the team's loss at Cincinnati the previous week. He twice challenged calls in that game, and both went against the Ravens.

But the Ravens again lost out on a pair of challenges in the Denver game. Tight end Todd Heap appeared to have a touchdown catch, and officials reversed the touchdown call, agreeing with the Broncos' claim that he didn't catch it. The Ravens later lost out on another challenge involving Heap.

Billick was happy after the game with the team's victory but clearly upset about the calls. One of the first questions in the postgame press conference involved the instant replay.

Lights, camera, action.

"I quit. I give up," Billick said while looking to the sky in clear exasperation. "I've tried to be an advocate for the instant replay. I've tried to do the company line. I've said the right things. Dump the whole fucking thing."

That caught everyone's attention. But the coach went on.

"We have spent so much money on this thing and it doesn't work. I've tried. League, I'm sorry, I've tried to hold up and hold the line. Dump it. Get rid of the whole damn thing because it doesn't work. It doesn't work. Move on."

Billick then addressed it again at his usual Monday press conference—his use of language, that is.

"I've got to start out and pay my penance and apologize for my language yesterday," he said. "Most of you were able to effectively bleep it out. Although, I find it interesting that as offensive as that is, that piece that gets bleeped keeps showing up over and over. They keep showing it. But for our radio in particular, I know that's not as filtered. Trust me, I'm paying my penance with my mother and my wife and my daughter, and will do so for quite a while, so I apologize for that."

Even coaches sometimes still must answer to their parents.

The Coach Who Kept Trying to Be Head Coach

Marvin Lewis was given a huge amount of credit for the defense's success in the 2000 season. The defensive coordinator helped put everything together, and Baltimore's defense was considered one of the best of all time.

They set a record for fewest rushing yards allowed in one season (970), and the Ravens then gave up only 258 yards on the ground in the four playoff wins. The Ravens also stopped teams passing. There was very little that teams could do to crack the Baltimore defense.

Most people thought that Lewis was a lock to get a head coaching job right away. But it didn't happen, although he came close. Lewis came back to the Ravens for 2001 and just missed on a head coaching job the following year. Lewis then said he'd return to Baltimore again before suddenly changing his mind and going to Washington to be the defensive coordinator under then-coach Steve Spurrier.

Lewis finally got his head coaching job when he took over the Cincinnati Bengals after the 2002 season.

The Ravens were very happy that Lewis finally got a chance they felt he deserved long before.

"Marvin is so deserving of this opportunity, and I am so happy that it came through and developed for him in Cincinnati," Modell said. "I have been active for several years on his behalf for him to get a head coaching job in the NFL. He and his family deserve the best, and I look forward to seeing what he can accomplish as a head coach."

Both Billick and Newsome each said they were glad Lewis finally got a head coaching job and thought he'd be successful.

"Marvin has served his apprenticeship," Newsome said. "He's worked hard to become a head coach in the NFL. I'm excited that he's getting this great opportunity. I don't have any doubts that he will have success."

Billick said it was "long overdue...he is going to help them win. I know he'll do a great job." The interesting part was that Cincinnati beat the Ravens early in the season and then had to come to Baltimore for a key late-season game. The Ravens scored a 31-13 victory over their old defensive coordinator's team.

Marvin Lewis handled the loss in his old home ballpark with grace when talking after the game. When asked about a defense that he had helped build, Lewis deflected the question.

"Well, don't give me credit; give those guys over there [credit]," Lewis said. "[Defensive coordinator] Mike Nolan and his staff [should get] credit, because they're doing a hell of a job, and they won today."

A Quiet Replacement

Lewis had gained a huge amount of media notice while the Ravens' defense became nationally known during their Super Bowl run in 2000 and wild card playoff appearance the next year.

Lewis's replacement was much quieter, but has become just as well respected. Mike Nolan has rebuilt the Baltimore defense with different players and in a different style that let the Ravens become dominant once again.

Nolan is a much more low-key personality than Lewis was while with the Ravens. He's been an NFL assistant for 17 years and changed the Ravens from a 4-3 style to mostly a 3-4. The entire defensive line is different from the Super Bowl championship team, while just one starter remains in the secondary.

They built the defense around the linebackers like Lewis and Boulware, both of whom played key roles in the championship team. Baltimore's defense was ranked third overall in the NFL in 2003 and tied for first in the AFC and second in the NFL with 41 takeaways.

The Ravens' defense didn't allow a touchdown in five games this season, and it kept getting better throughout the year.

"It's hard to find defensive coordinators who trust their players," said Ray Lewis. "I am talking about the players who he knows are going to put in the work and come to work every day. He gives you the flexibility to go play football. When you see Mike talk, he is very energetic. When you see that in a coach, that gives energy to the players. I don't know if Mike is too far from Marvin. The way they speak, their terminology—it's almost identical."

Nolan remained low-key from the start. He came to the Ravens and coached the wide receivers in 2001 before taking over for Marvin Lewis the following year. He said that coming up with a flexible defense has been a key to Baltimore's success in the last two years—despite being such a very young team.

"It's a neat thing to be able to design something for the player to take advantage of," Nolan said. "It's trying to put them in a position to utilize their strengths rather than say [that] this is our defense, and we're going to do it this way because that's what I know. That's narrow-minded and doesn't allow players to shine."

Nolan, whose father, Dick, was an NFL head coach (New Orleans, San Francisco) is likely to become a head coach within the next few years, especially if the Baltimore defense continues to improve as it has.

Oops

The Ravens have taken some criticism over the past few years for their trash-talking and not being afraid to run their mouths. But it was the Tennessee Titans who pulled a stunt that proved costly during the 2000 season.

Baltimore went to Tennessee for the second-round AFC playoff game in 2000. But the Titans put a message on their video screen before the game labeled as a "Special Message from Brian Billick and the Baltimore Ravens."

It showed Billick after the Ravens beat Tennessee earlier that season saying that Baltimore was the better team. The video fired up Tennessee's crowd and infuriated the Ravens.

Several of the Ravens said afterward that the Titans could have used better timing with something like that, but Billick tried to play it down. Regardless, it definitely helped fire up a Ravens team that didn't need any extra fire on this particular day.

The Hall of Fame Coach

Billick always has found solid assistant coaches for his team. He likes good teachers to show the players the right way to play the game.

He found a very good teacher in 2003 when hiring Hall of Fame linebacker Mike Singletary to coach the team's linebackers. The move worked nicely as the linebackers turned in an extraordinary season, helping the defense carry a big part of the load on the division championship team.

Singletary was widely recognized as one of the NFL's top linebackers during his career with the Chicago Bears. He became the cornerstone of the team's 46 defense that ran roughshod through the NFL during the 1985 season.

Singletary is a man of great commitment and honor and is very well respected throughout the NFL. He hadn't coached in the league yet, but quickly fit into a Baltimore team trying to rebuild parts of its defense.

Ray Lewis, as always, led the linebackers. He was ecstatic to get Singletary as his coach and smiled every time someone asked about what it was like to play for the Hall of Famer.

"As a coach, he is truly heaven-sent," Lewis said. "I want to take away from him anything he can teach me. I always respected him. He looks directly at you when he talks. Eye to eye, man to man. It's heartwarming. He's there for you."

Billick wanted a big name to help coach the Lewis-led linebackers, and Singletary turned out to be the right choice as he became very popular with those players.

"You just don't bring in anybody to coach Ray Lewis," Billick said. "The respect these guys have for one another on and off the field, what Mike Singletary represents to Ray Lewis. Mike's becoming a very good coach, he's going to be a great coach and has a long time in this league if that's what he chooses to do."

It would take the world's greatest detective to find anyone in the National Football League who'd say anything bad about Singletary. He has about a clean a reputation as is possible. As a player, he made 1,488 tackles during his career with the Bears (1981-1992) and was twice named the league's Defensive Player of the Year. He also was picked three times as the National Football Conference's Player of the Year before being voted into the Hall of Fame in 1998.

In addition, Singletary was picked as the 1990 NFL Man of the Year for the combination of abilities on the field and contributions off it. His off-field work is well known, as Singletary is an impressive motivational speaker and talks about a variety of subjects—often stressing the importance of a father's responsibilities.

Singletary has written four books, including one in 2003 titled *On the Subject of Leadership*. He lives in a Baltimore suburb with his wife, Kim, and their seven children.

But he's very happy to be associated with football once again.

"I always wanted to coach, and when I played in the NFL, I prepared myself to coach by learning everything I possibly could from every angle of the defense," Singletary said. "What kept me from coaching were priorities, and that was my family. I've had several chances over the years, but decided to bypass them. Thankfully, I did, and it's helped me keep things in perspective."

Like Father, Like Son, Sort Of

Rex Ryan knows football. It's truly all in his family.

The Ravens' defensive line coach is the son of well known coach Buddy Ryan, who ran the defense of Chicago's 1985 Super Bowl championship team and later became the Philadelphia head coach.

Rex's brother, Rob, is the defensive coordinator of the Oakland Raiders. Rex Ryan has been with the Ravens since 1999 and has a Super Bowl ring from the win over the Giants.

Ryan has done a strong job with two different types of defensive lines. He ran the line from the strong 4-3 defense that helped the Ravens dismantle several offenses in the 2000 season. That line featured ends Michael McCrary and Rob Burnett plus massive tackles Tony Siragusa and Sam Adams.

But the team's salary cap problems and injuries forced all four players' Ravens careers to end shortly afterward. Ryan was forced to work with a very young line in 2002 and 2003, but it quickly grew into a strong part of the Baltimore defense.

The Ravens had switched to a 3-4 style under new coordinator Mike Nolan, and Ryan worked hard at getting good play from ends Anthony Weaver and Marques Douglas plus nose tackle Kelly Gregg. The strong defensive line play let linebackers Lewis, Boulware, Ed Hartwell and others run loose to stop other teams' offenses throughout the season.

"Rex is considered one of the best young defensive minds in the game today," said Billick in last summer's media guide. "He has a great rapport with his players. His enthusiasm is infectious. He gets a lot out of guys, and they love to play for him."

Matte's Musings on Rex Ryan and Other Things

"I'll tell you that Rex is a guy who doesn't get, in my opinion, the kudos he should get. He's a knowledgeable coach. He's a guy who really knows how to move his players around. I interview him all the time. I like to talk to him. I think Rex has just been fundamentally a great defensive coach. I think he's done an outstanding job this year. He's got Kelly Gregg, Marques Douglas and Terrell Suggs and guys like that.

"I like the job that Rex has done. He's done such a great job with these guys. Douglas shoots the gap, he does it all. Gregg is a no-name guy who's got great balance and does a lot of things. Maake Kemoeatu also is strong—you take a look at these guys, the no-name group, but yet they've done an absolutely outstanding job.

"I sit down after every game and I have a conversation with Rex and Donnie Henderson [former assistant coach who left after the season to go to the Jets]. I talk to these guys; I like the way they coach. They're hands-on guys. We sit on the bus and review the whole game, explain what they did. It helps me understand what the hell is going on and gives me insight. I get some great insight and get a look at the game plan.

"Before the Bengals game here in Baltimore, I asked Rex if they were going to come after Jon Kitna. He said, "I'd like to come after him a little bit, but I don't think we're going to have to because we did such a good job with the four-man rush last time that we're just going to drop back in coverage because they've got good coverage." In other words, the Ravens tricked the Bengals a little. Suggs and Boulware still got all over them.

Adding Some Help Quietly

Jim Fassel was the head coach of the Giants team that the Ravens beat in Super Bowl XXXIV. Fassel had been respected for many years as a strong offensive coach—he played a big role in rejuvenating the careers of John Elway and Kerry Collins—and Baltimore needed some kind of offensive spark.

Fassel and Billick had been close friends for a while. Interestingly, for all of the teasing that Billick takes about having a big ego, it's impressive for a head coach to bring in a former head coach to help with his team's offense.

It also quietly gave somewhat embattled offensive coordinator Matt Cavanaugh a boost. Billick handled it quietly enough so that it didn't look like the move was made to help a struggling offensive coordinator but simply to help the team.

Fassel made it clear at the press conference that he's looking at becoming a head coach in the NFL once more, but that coming to Baltimore felt right.

"I think this is the right thing for me," Fassel said. "I'd love to help [Brian]. I'll grow a lot by not having the heavy stress and pressure...and maybe broaden my scopes and help Brian. This is a perfect, perfect, perfect situation for me to get some time off and help a great friend."

Fassel is set to be in Baltimore with the team the first three days of the week before heading back home and working on the next week's game.

"Matt Cavanaugh played for Jim, so Matt sees this as nothing but a positive," Billick said. "I've been known to do things unconventionally."

Billick and the Ravens heard plenty of heat throughout 2003, and a few previous seasons, about their offensive problems. Many said that the Ravens had a very plain offense that didn't do much or give the team a chance to score points. The addition of Fassel should help.

Matte's Musings on Fassel and the Offense

"Fassel, now that's a good move. That's a nice one. He's got a great friendship with Billick. I like Fassel, and I think he's a class act. He's just a good person. He and Billick are good friends. That's what the buddy system is all about. If you take a look around the NFL, once you get in and crack the skin of the NFL and you get inside there, these coaches move around to different teams. It can only enhance the offense, I think. He'll come up with some good ideas, and we need it. You're not putting offensive coordinator Matt Cavanaugh down by any means, but you're just saying I'm going to give Cavanaugh some help. Billick is doing it the polite way, the diplomatic way. That's the way he is. It will keep Fassel busy, keep him active in football. I think Fassel will help us. How can he hurt us? This team has got to develop some kind of offensive strategy that will work. I think that any new idea will make a difference, but it's the idea of 'How do you execute?' You can come up with all kinds of game plans, but if you don't have the receivers to go out there and run the pass patterns and catch the football and get the ball to them…you've got the running game, that's established, that's a known entity. But you still have to get the ball down the field, and hey, it's good to help us. There's no question about that. Billick's saying that Boller will be the quarterback in the off season is good, because you don't want any indecision. I think Billick is a very strong-minded guy. He knows what he wants to do, and he'll implement that plan."

Helping in a Quiet Way

Football takes up a whole lot of time in Matt Simon's life. The Ravens' running backs coach works countless hours preparing for the week's game and in the off season getting ready for the upcoming season.

But Simon has added another football task to his plate. He helped start a team in Howard County in the Mid-Atlantic Unlimited Youth Football Association. Founded by Baltimore's Bill Casagrande, the league specializes in getting boys who might be too big in the weight and size restrictions of other leagues a chance to play the game.

Simon first had a personal interest when his son, Aaron, who was taller and bigger, needed a place to play a few years ago. Aaron was five foot six and 160 pounds at the age of 11, and Simon began searching.

He found the MUYFA and helped start a team in Howard County for 11-14 year olds in 2001.

"Some of the children were ostracized, being in programs that had weight stipulations," Simon said. "We put a very difficult yoke on them emotionally."

Simon wanted the league to have some sympathy for the bigger kids, who often are pushed aside or laughed at for being too big.

"They are made to feel different when, deep in their minds, they feel they belong," Simon said.

Simon pushed hard to get the league started and set up. He's the team's president/general manager and helps raise about $10,000 annually for the team and works hard at doing many things without publicity.

He'll often bring players out to the team, like offensive linemen Ogden and Mulitalo, to talk to the kids. And despite being an NFL assistant coach, Simon keeps his eye on what's happening with the league.

The Bruins have a 28-player varsity, using players from sixth through the eighth grades, plus a 36-player J.V. That's for younger and more inexperienced players.

Simon is very sensitive to this time in children's lives. He wants them to have positive experiences while playing in this football program.

"The middle school age is really, really important," Simon said. "[This program] creates value to working with others and cooperating and working with a cause."

Chapter 4

RAY LEWIS

The Cornerstone

Many who watch the Baltimore Ravens will see Ray Lewis before anyone else. The talented linebacker catches the attention of fans and cameras with his frenzied pregame dance ritual and catches the attention of his teammates with his frenzied style on the field during the game.

Lewis has been the team leader on defense almost since his first game in 1996 when he came to Baltimore as a late first-round draft pick. The Ravens picked another franchise cornerstone, Jonathan Ogden, with their initial first-round pick that year and grabbed Lewis with their second.

Both turned out to be spectacular choices, but Lewis has gotten the most attention. Lewis has led the team in tackles each year—except for 2002 when he missed several games with a shoulder injury—and gives the Ravens something very unique on the field and in the locker room.

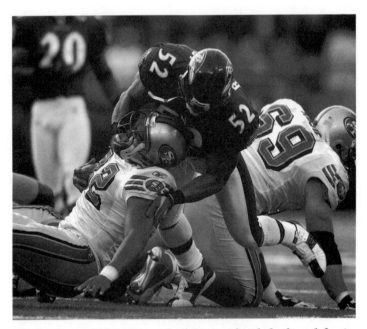

Ray Lewis reminds a 49er why he's considered the best defensive player in the NFL. (Photo by Mitchell Layton)

"There is no second speed for Ray," said Art Modell. "It's all out. He's as good a middle linebacker as I've ever seen. The only one who can give him a run for his money would be his coach, Mike Singletary."

Lewis quietly became a team leader during his rookie season. The Ravens were truly in a transition year as the team was in its first year after moving from Cleveland, and the defense was one of the NFL's worst.

But Lewis got off to a great start. During the team's first game ever as the Baltimore Ravens, Lewis had nine tackles and an interception in the end zone in the 19-14 victory over the Oakland Raiders.

Lewis earned AFC Defensive Player of the Week honors for that first game. He finished his rookie season with a team-high

142 tackles despite missing over two games with injuries. Lewis then led the NFL with 210 tackles in his second year and made the Pro Bowl again.

After that, Lewis made the Pro Bowl four more consecutive years before the shoulder injury shelved him for 11 games in 2002.

And that gave him something different to prove in 2003. Could he come back and be the player he was before the injury and the subsequent shoulder surgery?

That's why making the Pro Bowl in 2003 and helping the Ravens win the AFC North for the first time meant so much to the linebacker.

"I always say one thing," Lewis said. "You can question my ability, but you can't question my heart. Coming off the shoulder surgery, [making the Pro Bowl] was one of the things I dreamed of."

Number 52 Leads a Younger Group

Lewis gave the media a good look at his tough leadership style midway through the 2003 season as the Ravens were trying to take control of the division after struggling in recent games.

The Ravens were 5-4 and in first place with a one-game lead over Cincinnati. Quarterback Anthony Wright was set to make his Ravens debut against Miami, and many were questioning when Baltimore would fall.

And Lewis was tired of hearing it. So before practice one day, Lewis expressed his frustrations to the media.

"When we lost that first week against Pittsburgh, everybody wrote us off," Ray Lewis said before the St. Louis game several days earlier "'Oh, the Steelers are going to win this.' They're [3-6] right now, and any way you want to look at it, we're leading our division. So anybody who wants to deal with us and are on our schedule, come deal with us. It's simple."

What's also simple is how Lewis sets the tone. The hard-working linebacker makes plays from sideline to sideline and serves as an inspiration to his defensive teammates with his in-your-face style. It sparks those around him constantly.

The Ravens use a different defense than the one many felt was among the best of all time in 2000 when Baltimore won the Super Bowl. Singletary now coaches the linebackers, and defensive coordinator Mike Nolan installed a 3-4 defense that relied heavily on younger players like Terrell Suggs, Ed Hartwell, Kelly Gregg, Adalius Thomas, and Tony Weaver up front while using ballhawks Ed Reed and Gary Baxter to shut down opposing receivers.

But the team's defense, with all of its talent, has Lewis as its centerpiece. That's something everyone agrees with and no one will dispute.

"How can you not look up to a guy that's been to the Pro Bowl, a guy that's been the Super Bowl MVP, a guy that's been on top?" Hartwell asks. "You ask how did he do it [and] how can I do it? It's going to be a long day for offenses [because] they're going to go home with bruises. We grow every day and bond together and before it's over, we'll dominate."

Lewis pushes the defense, which is one of the NFL's youngest, at a relentless pace. He simply wants the Ravens to play their best and works so hard that everyone follows suit. They really have no choice.

"He's always been a guy who leads by example," teammate Marques Douglas said. "When it's a fourth-and-one situation, you can look into his eyes and you can see that fire, and you don't want to let a guy like that down."

Lewis won't even talk about failure. He loves the fact that so many in the NFL overlooked the Ravens because they thought the team was too young. Lewis simply smiles when talking

Lewis brings a high level of intensity to his celebrations. (Photo by Mitchell Layton)

about his team being overlooked. After all, he's been there before.

"Nobody ever thought the Ravens were going to be here," Lewis said. "They didn't think we were going to be here in 2000, but guess what? We're back again."

The Ray Lewis Problems

Nearly everyone who follows NFL football knows about the problems that Lewis experienced in the months following the 1999 season—the off-field crises that drew national attention.

Lewis was initially facing murder charges stemming from the death of two men after a street fight in Atlanta on January 31, 2000. The case received a huge amount of national publicity that hurt Lewis's reputation—especially considering the fact that there were several pictures of him in a jail jumpsuit.

But after a long and tough process for Lewis, the murder charges against the linebacker were withdrawn in midtrial at the prosecutor's initiative. Still, the NFL hit Lewis with a large fine of $250,000 for conduct detrimental to the league.

In the end, Lewis pleaded guilty to just one misdemeanor count of obstruction of law enforcement officers and interference with a law enforcement investigation. He also was sentenced to one year's probation and had to pay some court costs.

Lewis and his attorney, Ed Garland, had strongly argued that the charges were without basis from the beginning and repeatedly pushed Atlanta officials to drop the charges. But it wasn't until about the midway point in the trial that the prosecution cut a deal with Lewis and finally withdrew the murder charges.

Lewis didn't say much until coming back to Baltimore in early June, 2000, for a wide-ranging press conference with Modell, Garland, and others.

Lewis was clearly upset, angered and frustrated at the news conference. His first statements clearly show that.

"How I feel...I'm tired. I'm exhausted. I've been through something in my life that I've never been through before. I've faced fourth downs and ones a lot of times before, and I have guys that know I'm going to step up in that position. But when it's fourth down and life, you don't know what to do in that situation. And that's what happened when the police approached me and I gave a false statement to them. When you're dealing with fourth and life, you never know what you're going to do.

"I'm angry. I'm mad at myself for the situation I put my family in. I take all responsibility for that. My teammates, my fans, especially...while in jail. I received so much mail...that was one of my daily routines, was to sit up and listen and read what people wrote to me in jail. Two weeks in jail is hard."

Garland clearly believed in Lewis from the start. He said that Lewis repeatedly told him that he was innocent right from the beginning and never changed.

Garland explained to the media that the charges of murder, aggravated assault, and felony murder were completely dropped. The misdemeanor wasn't part of a plea bargain but something a little different.

"The ball started rolling against Ray Lewis in the beginning," Garland said that night. "The fact that he was a celebrity and they had focused on Ray Lewis caused them to shape, look at and try to investigate to get a result...but then as [the prosecutor] really got the facts, as he really looked at the evidence, as he really reflected on it, he began to change."

Changing the Image

Many people felt that Lewis's image was permanently tarnished from the problems involving the murder charges and that his ability to make money off the field in the world of advertising and marketing would be permanently hurt.

But, interestingly, that's not what happened.

The best thing that happened to Lewis was that the Ravens won the Super Bowl the following season—with the linebacker winning nearly every award possible and becoming very well known for his play on the field. Still, when Lewis won the Super Bowl MVP award, he did not get the well known Disney World commercial given the game's award winner—quarterback Trent Dilfer got it instead.

Lewis also kept his image clean off the field during this time. He stayed away from all trouble and became known as arguably the best player in the NFL.

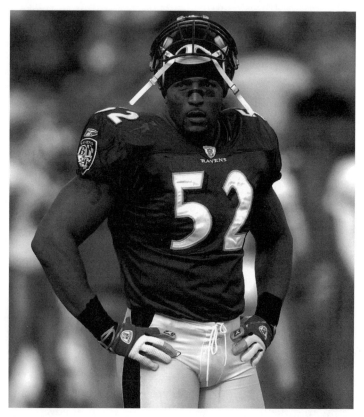

In recent years, Lewis has been able to move past some off-the-field problems and become a popular athlete for endorsements. (Photo by Mitchell Layton)

But everything started changing about a year and a half ago, according to a December, 2003 *Baltimore Business Journal* article. Robert J. Terry's story said that things began to move in a different direction when Lewis was picked to be in commercials for video game developer EA Sports.

The commercials were well received and went through the season. Lewis also wound up in print and television spots for Reebok and NFL Equipment. They also came out very well.

"He embodies one of the core messages we have in our brand campaign, which is 'outperform,'" John Lynch, Reebok's vice president of sports marketing, said in Terry's story. "It's hard to say there's a better player on the football field."

The EA Sports spots were comedic ones that featured Lewis making life somewhat difficult for some NFL players rookies. The popular commercial turned out very funny.

"Obviously, there was more than a little bit of concern," said Sandy Sandoval, director of athletic relations for EA Sports. "But I looked at the writing for a few of the spots and I just thought, 'This is Ray Lewis.' When I met with him, I just found him to be a sincere guy, a very articulate young man. Then I had to get it past our executive people, explaining that it's not just a good opportunity for Ray, but a great opportunity for us."

Terry's article also talked about how Lewis was able to change the image from murder trial defendant to pitchman. Terry quoted Bob Williams, CEO of Burns Sports & Celebrities, an Illinois-based firm that hooks up endorsers with advertisers.

"He has made quite a comeback," said Williams in the article, noting his company does not work with Lewis. "A guy who was really persona non grata in terms of endorsements has turned it around in a big way."

Lewis now is becoming a regular on commercials in the Baltimore area, and it's likely that he'll be seen even more on spots regionally and nationally. It's one of the more amazing turnaround stories that sports advertising has seen in a long time.

Matte's Musings on Ray Lewis

"Geez, what can you say about Ray Lewis? He just leads by example. He works so hard during the season and during the off season. How he stays in total condition and he's focused. How much time he spends in the classroom studying. I was so impressed with him and I'm even more impressed now since 2000 with how he's improved on his pass coverage, how he gets back in the drops knowing where the guys are coming from. He has that feel. It's just like Ed Reed. He'll be a Hall of Famer. If he doesn't get hurt, he'll be a Hall of Famer. In college, you have like a 10-game schedule, now you're doubling. You're playing 20 games when they get to the pros. You run out of gas because your body is not used to it.

"What you have to do is what Ray Lewis does. He stays in shape all year long. He was a leader at the beginning. Ray was a little sluggish the first four or five games, and then he learned how to condition himself to play that position much better. Ray increased his speed by stretching and doing the proper exercises. He was sort of bulked up when he first came in here. I took my grandson and son with me before a scrimmage at the stadium before preseason started. We went down on the field and we talked to Art Modell and Kyle Boller. Then out comes Ray Lewis. My son said, "God, he looks like he's really in great shape." I told him that he's got just six percent body fat. Wow. My son thought that was just great.

"But Ray also changed his image since all the trouble he got into, he's worked very, very, very hard at that. Ray learned to let it go. That's what people don't understand. You're part of a group that protects each other. Ray came up in a pretty tough neighborhood. It's a very close-knit thing, and to break that is hard. I think Ray has gotten away from that. I think he's improved his image so much corporately. I believe he did it with some great guidance from Art Modell. Sharpe really helped. He had the class. He had the experience, and he was a much more mature guy—and very, very articulate. He just had a presence. I always thought he was the most profound influence on him because trouble will find you. I had a really short fuse. I can tell you stories that happened that the press would have loved. But it's a different time now. Ray has got to weigh what he does, and he's doing a better job of that now. Now everybody's looking for it because these guys are making so much money. As for Ray, I said a lot of things publicly supporting him. It was wrong place, wrong time, wrong people. And I backed him and Ray came up to me and said, 'I want to thank you for your support.' I just said wrong place, wrong time, trying to keep his friends out of trouble."

Chapter 5

THE SUPER BOWL SEASON

No Touchdowns, No Problem

The defense got loads of national attention in 2000, as many felt it was the best of all time. In fact, the defense was the main reason the Ravens won the Super Bowl.

But the offense earned plenty of attention that season—for different reasons. The Baltimore offense endured a five-game streak without a touchdown. The Ravens didn't score a touchdown throughout the month of October, losing three of five games.

The offensive problems forced Billick to change quarterbacks. He shifted from the inconsistent Tony Banks to Trent Dilfer. Despite no touchdowns, Baltimore won two of the games in the streak, beating Cleveland and Jacksonville on the road, using nine field goals from Matt Stover.

The Ravens then lost to Washington, Pittsburgh and Tennessee before Dilfer finally broke the infamous streak with a

14-yard touchdown pass to Brandon Stokley that sparked a 27-7 victory over Cincinnati.

Interestingly enough, it was Stokley's first catch of the season—and just the second of his career.

Matte's Musings on the Super Bowl Defense

"They were just so damn good. At defensive end, Rob Burnett was one of the true leaders of the team, in my opinion. He was a guy who led by example. He kept the practices going well, and he was a class act. Rob was a guy I had a lot of respect for because he always was giving you 150 percent on every play. Go to the other defensive end with Mike McCrary and it's the same thing. He was a loner. We did some broadcasting with him this year, and he's quiet. It's hard to bring things out. He doesn't like to talk about himself. Michael was really a cheerleader on the field. He had a different motor inside of him on game day. Different players have different motors. I'd relate him to a Deacon Jones from the Rams when I played. He had that motor going all the time. You just knew he was going to come after you. I don't think there was ever a time when Michael was in there that he didn't give you 150 percent on the defense.

"Then you take the two internal guys they had in there, Siragusa and Adams, those two guys occupied three people. What that did was sort of let the linebackers rove around. That's why Ray Lewis had such a great, great year, because Sam Adams or the Goose would engage the center and the guard, both of them, and the other one would take either the guard and that collapses the middle, and Ray's just peeling off and going. I'm still a firm believer that you have to have the big guys in there, but I'm being disproved this year by Kelly Gregg. Here's a guy

Sam Adams made plays and provided veteran leadership during the Ravens' remarkable Super Bowl season. (Photo by Phil Hoffmann)

who's six foot and 310 pounds, and he's got a great build and great strength.

"But Adams and Goose were so big that you couldn't push them around. They would stay there so that the middle linebacker, Boulware, and Jamie Sharper could do what they needed. Jamie was just great. Both had great families, and both were very pointed in what they wanted to do. I don't think that Peter Boulware has reached his potential yet. I think that Peter is sort of a rangy kind of linebacker, sort of like a Ted Hendricks. I think Peter will get better as he gets older like Ted. The given is that Ray gets to sort of do what he wants to do out there. What Boulware has to do is stay at home and wait, and then the plays come to his side; he gets to make the play. And with Jamie Sharper, he became better each year. The one thing that Art Modell and Ozzie and Phil Savage have done is gone out and gotten some good athletes, and they can do a lot of things. Jamie Sharper had great speed; Peter Boulware wasn't the fastest of all. These guys could get back into pass coverage, and they understood the defense. They believed in Marvin Lewis's defense. When they first came up here, Marvin grabbed hold of them, took them and developed them. And before Marvin, they had Maxie Baughan. He was one of the smartest football players I played against in my life.

"But Marvin Lewis, he was low-profile. He would say, 'All I do is coach, and players play.' He understood the other team's offense, and he knew what he had to do to be able to stop the big things that the other team's offense had to do. He got the team believing in his system. Once they started that momentum going, and you had leaders like Ray Lewis and Rob Burnett and the Goose in there, it got started. Adams, well, Sam was like Dr. Jekyll and Mr. Hyde. He had an unusual personality, but was the complete football player. Then when he came in here, Sam started proving himself. I had that same drive as a player. I went to the Pro Bowl a few times, but you always have that drive to say, 'I want my peers to identify me.' That's Sam Adams, and I think he deserved to be identified because he played good, sound football.

"He came in with the reputation of being a pain in the butt. He came in here and he saw that defense and his eyes lit up. If you're a defensive player, to get to play with that defense? I think that changed him. He came out with a great attitude. When the bell rang, he was out on the field giving 100 percent. He could be anything he wants to be; it's just how they want to use him."

In the Middle of the Night, I Go Walking in My Sleep

There were some local fans who wanted to greet the Ravens when they returned from their AFC championship game victory over Oakland. But here was the problem—the team wouldn't return until the middle of the night. Well, that's no problem, thought a bunch of fans.

About 1,500 fans lined the road across from the team's training complex and waited for the team. They stood on the side of the quiet road in the rain and cold and simply waited. The color purple was everywhere. Most people wore Ravens shirts or hats or jackets. They carried signs with some reference to the upcoming Super Bowl and basically celebrated.

In fact, the celebration went on in many ways. There's a small shopping strip directly across from the team's training facility in Owings Mills, and a couple of eating places actually opened up around midnight and were serving food as late as 3 a.m.

The businesses were making a nice little killing on this night, selling pizzas, subs, ice cream and all kinds of food. People sat inside the places and waited and talked Ravens football for hours. For a while, some of the fans came in to simply get out of the rain that never seemed to stop—after all, who's going to eat pizza at 1:45 a.m.? But they eventually gave in and grabbed some food.

But the eating was just to kill time until the traveling party returned home. The crowd somehow kept finding out the status of where the Ravens were. The word eventually got around that the team would get back to the training complex around 3-3:30 a.m.

The crowd kept growing, almost by the minute. It was easy to walk around at 1 a.m. Some people were even playing catch with a football by the side of the road. But as 3 a.m. drew closer, the crowd began getting more fired up. There were fans who had been waiting for more than seven hours, drinking coffee and other, um, beverages, to keep warm. The chant "Su-per Bowl, Su-per Bowl" droned on endlessly.

And then it happened. The 13-vehicle convoy that included three team buses made its way into the team's training complex at around 3:04 a.m., setting off an incredible roar from the crowd. There may have been 1,500 people, but the noise truly sounded like 15,000.

The players loved it. Many got right off the team bus and jumped into their cars in the parking lot that's only about 100 yards off the road behind the main entrance. Others surprised many of the fans by talking with them and whipping out their own video cameras and filming the celebration. Then the players slowly drove their cars out of the entrance, turned onto the main road and filmed the fans—often thanking them for their support.

Lional Dalton, who now plays for the Washington Redskins, used his right hand to steer his car while videotaping with his left hand and talking and laughing with the fans who were in the front row on the left side of the road. Other players began helping the fans by chanting "Su-per Bowl, Su-per Bowl."

One overanxious parent actually pushed his elementary school-age son down so he could reach over and pick up something one of the players dropped from his car. The kid nearly rolled into the path of the car, but the father simply giggled like a fool.

But that's the way things went on this night. Even Billick waved to the fans. He had his window down and he looked at the several media people in the front row. When asked about the wild amount of noise being made at 3:30 a.m., Billick simply smiled.

"It sounds great to me," Billick said.

The Pre-Super Bowl Rally

The Ravens left for the Super Bowl on January 22. It was a very cold and sunny morning, a typical winter's day in Baltimore. But before they left, the Ravens held a huge rally at the Inner Harbor, a popular shopping and tourist attraction right up the street from their stadium.

Many Ravens fans skipped work to get there and listen to several of the players give their thoughts before the team headed for Tampa. The crowd loved hearing anyone connected with the team—a ball boy would have gotten a standing ovation by this point—but as usual, Ray Lewis got the biggest reaction.

Showing up in a slick suit, Lewis got the crowd roaring with the chant he gave the team that had now become famous. He asked the crowd if it was ready and then took off. "What time is it? Game time. What time is it? Game time. Are my dogs in the house? Woo, woo, woo, woo."

The crowd went bananas. And it was off to Tampa.

Brian Billick took the focus off Ray Lewis early in the week before the Super Bowl. (Photo by Mitchell Layton)

How to Take the Heat off Your Best Player in Front of the National Media in One Easy Step

Billick is a master at working with the press. He knows how to pull the strings and get his message across—whatever it is. But his best effort might have come when addressing the national media in Tampa after the Ravens arrived for the Super Bowl.

There was no doubt that Ray Lewis and his problems the previous year would come up for discussion. Probably many times. Billick didn't want that to become a distraction on the week of the team's biggest game, so he quickly took care of that.

He stood up in front of the national media at a press conference and made his thoughts very clear.

"Before you ask any questions, I know the Giants will have a curfew," Billick said. "We will not. I know you are going to ask Ray and me a lot of questions. He answered all those questions last June. Just because someone wants to ask about it again doesn't mean that Ray or I, or any of the Ravens, have to address it again."

That surprised many members of the media because coaches and players usually are happy and don't want to cause trouble. Billick made several more statements along those lines during the press conference. And he was right, Lewis was bombarded with questions from the media about what had happened in Atlanta. But Lewis handled it well, and the issue didn't cause any problems.

Many felt that Billick's blunt statement to the national media at the start of the week took a lot of the pressure off Lewis because media people were talking as much about how surprising it was that a coach would talk like that as about what the linebacker had been accused of. That's how to work the media. And it worked perfectly.

Festivus Maximus

Billick wanted the team to remain focused during the regular season even as they slowly became playoff contenders. To that end, no one was allowed to say the word "playoffs," or as he called it, "the P-word," until the team had clinched a spot—or they would face a fine from the coaching staff.

But the players wanted to say something, and the term "Festivus" began being used when talking about the playoffs.

Players used it constantly. "Festivus Maximus" became the phrase used when discussing the later rounds of the playoffs, like the Super Bowl. The players loved saying both things, and the slogans caught on like wildfire in Baltimore.

However, the word "playoffs" still couldn't be used. That's when marketing took over. A friend of guard Edwin Mulitalo came up with an idea for T-shirts with the substitute phrase and/or phrases.

Mulitalo took it one step further and marketed T-shirts he designed saying "Festivus" and "Festivus Maximus." They sold like wildfire and people are still wearing them around town three years later.

Billick's banning of the "P-word" appeared to be a strategy to keep his team focused. The Ravens had never been in real contention for the playoffs before the 2000 season, and Billick didn't want the players talking about it and getting too concerned with making the postseason play and thinking about it.

It was a good strategy, because when the players would joke around and say the word "Festivus" in talking to the media, everyone knew what they were saying—and not saying. There were a lot of laughs from it, and both players and coaches enjoyed it.

Billick especially had some fun with it at the right times. When the Ravens clinched their first playoff spot with a 24-3 victory over San Diego on a cold day in Baltimore in Game 14, Billick gave the perfect quote.

"Obviously, the fine for the P-word is off," Billick said. "We earned the right to say we're a playoff team. We now have the right to say we want to go to the Super Bowl. No Festivus. No Festivus Maximus. Super Bowl."

Peter Boulware and the Ravens' defense, which was amazing during the regular season, was even better during the playoffs, never giving up more than 10 points to any of their four opponents. (Photo by Mitchell Layton)

Super Bowl Surprise

Winning Super Bowl XXXV in Tampa Bay was the franchise's biggest moment for several reasons.

First, capturing any type of championship is always spectacular, but it's even more fun when no one expects you to do so. Since coming to Baltimore in 1996, the Ravens' best record was an 8-8 finish the year before in Brian Billick's first season as head coach.

And the team suffered through a five-week stretch earlier in that year where they couldn't score a touchdown and had to change quarterbacks. But the Ravens got everything turned around after that midseason stumble that left them with a 5-4 record and many questioning their offense.

They cut down on the mistakes, and the defense moved up to a near legendary status. The Baltimore defense gave up only 59 rushing first downs in the team's 16 games—and just 970 yards overall—and helped support an offense that struggled at times.

But everything came together and the team won its final seven regular-season games to roll into the playoffs with a 12-4 record. The Ravens then routed Denver, 21-3, in the first playoff game before heading to Tennessee and using some blocked kicks and big plays to pull out a 24-10 victory over the rival Titans.

Backup defensive lineman Keith Washington blocked two Al Del Greco field goals, and the second was picked up by reserve defensive back Anthony Mitchell and returned for a 90-yard touchdown with 12:12 left. That gave the Ravens a 17-10 lead.

The defense then came up with one more big play when Ray Lewis picked off a Steve McNair pass and rumbled on for a 50-yard touchdown about six minutes later for the final score. The Titans outgained the Ravens, 317-134, but came up short.

Baltimore then had little trouble in scoring a 16-3 victory over the Oakland Raiders in the AFC championship game. Tight end Shannon Sharpe turned a short pass on third and long into a 96-yard touchdown that gave the Ravens a 7-0 lead in the second quarter, and they never looked back.

Kicker Matt Stover added three field goals for the final score. Baltimore's tough defense roughed up and knocked out Oakland quarterback Rich Gannon and sent the team flying into the Super Bowl.

The big game belonged completely to the Ravens from start to finish. The New York Giants couldn't match Baltimore's speed, quickness, and intensity, and the Ravens rolled to a surprisingly easy 34-7 victory.

"You've done me proud," said an emotional Modell in the locker room after the game. "I can't tell you how proud I am of this organization...everybody. You've done me proud and I'll never forget it and I thank you."

Modell stood there fighting back tears for several moments while players and people with the organization filmed and took pictures and simply enjoyed the moment itself.

The Super Presents

The Modells had waited a long time for this and made sure everyone enjoyed it. They did something a bit unusual and gave presents to the traveling party when in Tampa Bay—on a regular basis.

"That was unexpected, but it's just strictly the way the Modells were," said Kevin Paige, now the assistant sports information director at Coppin State University in Baltimore but then an intern with the Ravens' public relations department. "They were very generous, and it made everyone feel great."

And the presents were not little things. The Ravens folks received video camcorders, digital cameras, sweatsuits, shirts, bags of full of merchandise, hats. Something was there every day, and everyone loved it. Players used the cameras and videos to record as much of that special week as they could.

Paige himself wound up working in the stadium's control room on game day, spotting for the stadium's public address announcer and being right in the middle of everything. He treasures the presents he received that week and still has every one of them.

The unusual part for him is that Paige had to turn down a Ravens internship during the summer of 1997 because he had already taken an internship with the *Milwaukee Journal*. But he got another internship in 2000 and got to stay with the team throughout the year.

He also got a trip to the Super Bowl plus some presents that made a journey to the big game that much more memorable.

One Big Play

Anthony Mitchell was a classic role player for the Baltimore Ravens' defense.

He played four seasons with the Ravens from 1999-2002 and played in 48 games. Mitchell started at times during the 2002 season as Baltimore was rebuilding its team following the off-season salary cap purge that cost the Ravens a number of key players.

But Mitchell is best known in Baltimore for one play, a play that might have given the Ravens the big spark during their Super Bowl run in 2000. Mitchell was on the field goal blocking team when the Ravens played at Tennessee and were locked in a 10-10 fourth-quarter tie.

The Titans tried to break the deadlock with a field goal, but Keith Washington of the Ravens blocked it. The ball came to Mitchell, who took off and ran for a 90-yard touchdown that gave Baltimore a 17-10 lead.

Ray Lewis later intercepted a Steve McNair pass and returned it for a touchdown for the 24-10 final score, but it was the Mitchell return that gave the Ravens the lead for good and pushed them into the AFC championship game.

A Tennessee field goal might have been enough to win the game, as the Ravens' offense was not moving at all on that afternoon. But Mitchell's play turned it around.

He stayed with the team through the 2002 season before getting traded to Jacksonville, where he played in 2003. In fact, Mitchell became a very valuable role player in Baltimore, but it was his one big play that Ravens fans will never forget.

Welcome Home to the Champs

The Ravens and the city scheduled a victory parade for the team—complete with a fleet of Hummers riding through downtown Baltimore—a few days after the Super Bowl victory.

But Mother Nature threw a wrench into the proceedings.

The weather was horrifying that day. It was cold and windy and rainy with the temperatures hovering in the 30s. Team officials wondered if they should talk to the city about cancelling the parade.

But people came despite the rotten weather. In fact, over 200,000 fans came out and braved the weather to greet the champions. The raincoats, umbrellas and hats were everywhere on this day. Even the players, coaches and team officials tried to stay dry, but no one really cared.

The event was televised live locally, preempting the talk shows. And no one cared. They just wanted to look at their champions. It had been over 17 years since Baltimore had a championship team, and that was the 1983 Orioles. The city hadn't celebrated a championship football team for 30 years.

That's a whole lot of emotion, and it all poured out that day. This city loved the Colts but never really had a chance to say goodbye. The city also needed a little time to take to the Ravens, but now the bond was formed. From this day forward, fans wore all kinds of purple Ravens clothes.

And they enjoyed themselves despite the weather. Ray Lewis fired up the crowd. So did Billick and Modell. David Modell showed the Vince Lombardi trophy, and everyone roared. The band was there—of course—and all kinds of Ravens shirts and hats were on display. This was a turning point in the franchise's history.

That's because no matter what happened, the Ravens had given Baltimore an emotional championship, something the city and its fans would never forget. And that's also why the weather didn't matter day.

Truth be told, the same number of fans might have come out even it was a blizzard.

Matte's Musings on the Super Bowl

"What a drive that was to get there. We just annihilated them. It wasn't even a game. We were such an intimidating defense that it was unbelievable, and then our special teams did such a great job in that game. And then the offense—Dilfer didn't make any mistakes, or just a few mistakes. It was just the accumulation of a lot of things that happened during the season that just came together. We were always the underdog. We were always looked down upon, and Billick played on that part of it. No respect, no respect, no respect. The defense said, 'What do you mean we have no respect? We'll go out and show them.' I can remember Ray Lewis saying, 'Get me one touchdown and we'll win the football game.' Matt Stover, what a class act he is, as far as sticking in here, and a real leader on this ball club. What I said early in the season was that this team looks like a team of destiny. Nobody's going to hold them back. They just kept on fighting and winning. They finally got the respect that was due. But you've got to give credit to the special teams. Look at Jermaine Lewis's touchdown return. He just had some great blocks there. There's such an emphasis by Billick and his coaching staff on special teams. That really helped in the Super Bowl, especially with Jermaine. The game was just total dominance, physical dominance. The defense took charge, and the offense came out there and did what it had to do. It wasn't spectacular, but it was fundamental. I was a little wary about the Giants because I thought there was a little—well, I still remember the Jets beating us when we were the big favorites. We were always the underdogs, but I thought there was this air of the Ravens walking out and saying, 'Hey, we'll be good, don't worry about it.' And they backed it up. I don't think there was a defense that I have ever seen, and I have talked to a lot of my compatriots about as this, but I'm telling you right now that the Ravens' defense dominated those games. They played fantastic. I'll put them down as probably the greatest all-time team defense that I've ever seen play."

Chapter 6

THE DEFENSE

The Sacker Who Got the Right Decision

Michael McCrary came to Baltimore without much fanfare, signing as a free agent before the 1997 season after four quiet years with Seattle and retiring during the 2002 season as one of the Ravens' top defensive linemen.

McCrary finished with 51 sacks for Baltimore during his six-year tenure, finally having to stop midway through 2002 when his knees couldn't take it any more. He had some incredible games for Baltimore, getting four sacks once, three sacks twice and 3.5 sacks another time.

But despite all of his success, McCrary was a soft-spoken guy who didn't get as much publicity because the defenses he played on had some real attention getters like Ray Lewis and Tony Siragusa.

However, McCrary did get some attention in a very big way in earlier days—much earlier. He was two years old when he became the plaintiff in a landmark integration civil rights lawsuit. His mother and father sued a non-integrated day care center that made no bones about the fact that they did not take African-American children.

The business claimed that being private exempted it from the 1964 Civil Rights Act. An article in *The Baltimore Sun* on May 22, 2001, talked about how Michael's parents, Sandy and Curtis McCrary, filed suit against the owners of Bobbie's Nursery School in Arlington, Virginia, in 1973.

The McCrarys won at the first level and then again in appeals court before the U.S. Supreme Court heard the case in the spring of 1976. The Court ruled 7-2 in favor of the McCrarys. That decision, according to *The Sun's* article "was a far-reaching milestone in civil rights, prohibiting discrimination

Mike McCrary's play always spoke volumes on the field. The courageous actions of his parents spoke volumes off the field. (Photo by Phil Hoffmann)

in all contracts, meaning virtually any monied transaction in the United States. It meant no vendors or service providers could discriminate on the basis of race."

In the article, McCrary said that his parents "stood up for what was right and came out with a very important win for minorities in this country. It's one of the reasons they're both heroes of mine."

The Retirement

McCrary truly was loved as a football player. He was a tough guy who worked hard, and the Ravens were sorry to lose McCrary when he finally made it official during the 2003 pre-season.

It was a tough decision for McCrary, who probably could have played a few more years if not for the knee problems. He was an old-school player who wanted to let his work speak for him.

"I can honestly say that I never took a play off," McCrary said at his retirement press conference. "I never wanted to be disappointed in the way that I played. Sometimes we'd lose, but I gave 100 percent. That's the way everyone should play, because you never know when the last game is going to be. It's really a special thing to be out there playing. That's in life, everything that you do, you should give 100 percent, try to be the best in whatever you do. I don't have any regrets at all."

The Ravens, by contrast, had plenty of regrets about losing someone who truly served as a leader of the defense during his tenure. That's why Modell, Billick, and others all showed up at the press conference to say an emotional goodbye.

"Over the years, you come across special performers, special people," Modell said. "When my story in the National Football League [is] written, there will be a whole chapter on this guy. I never saw or met a man more determined to be good, to be better, stay healthy, get healthy. [He was] committed to his craft, committed to his teammates, committed to me and the organization. He is one of a kind."

The team just loved him. Defensive assistant coach Rex Ryan barely got out a sentence before being unable to continue. But McCrary's words told the story of a person who just couldn't stop doing something he loved.

"It's been really difficult," he said. "My knees, as everybody knows, they have been bothering me. Doctors have told me that there is definitely no way that I should even consider playing again and that I should have stopped years ago. But it's been hard. I can't even watch a football game now, because I still have that fire inside of me. I guess the only way to quench it is to stay completely away from it, but it's hard. It was hard for me to come here today, because I have been trying to stay away from it."

The Hard Worker

Anthony Poindexter has been a graduate assistant with the Virginia football program for the past two years. As a coach, he's certainly got a few lessons to teach the Cavalier players.

Poindexter was scheduled to have been one of the top picks of the 1999 draft. Teams were drooling over the Virginia defensive back. He had it all—speed, quickness, the ability to cover, and brains.

Poindexter almost declared for the NFL draft after 1997, but stayed in college and was playing very well before suffering a career-threatening knee injury against North Carolina State. It all fell apart during the seventh game of Virginia's 1998 season. He tore three of the four ligaments in his knee on one play that ended his season and basically ruined his career. However, he was named the Atlantic Coast Conference's Defensive Player of the Year that season despite playing only six full games. He also earned the Brian Piccolo Award, given each year to the conference's most courageous player.

The injury basically scared off most NFL teams—except the Ravens. Poindexter needed to have total reconstructive knee surgery. An All-American each of the last two years in college, the Ravens thought Poindexter was progressing well in his rehabilitation and drafted him solely to look at the following year. Baltimore took a gamble and picked Poindexter in the seventh round of the 1999 draft, knowing that the defensive back still had a lot of rehab work in front of him.

"I told him I'm looking at the year 2000," Newsome said that day. "Anything we get out of him in the year 1999 will be a plus."

They didn't get anything in 1999 but certainly got something in 2000. Baltimore trainer Bill Tessendorf supervised a tough rehab program that Poindexter ground his way through. He made it back to the field for the 2000 season.

"I had worked all my life to get to this point, and my goal was to play in the NFL," Poindexter said in a recent interview. "I was there for two years in Baltimore—the second year I got to play. I really enjoyed it; I had no regrets about the decision I made."

Poindexter gives credit to the Baltimore staff for working tirelessly with a player simply trying his best to get back onto a football field once again.

"I enjoyed working with the trainers there," Poindexter said. "They really took care of me. I had a bad injury; I just didn't heal. I came back, but I was nowhere near the player I was before."

Poindexter worked hard and became a solid contributor on the Baltimore special teams and finished with 11 tackles and one forced fumble. He was occasionally deactivated for games, including the Super Bowl. But at season's end, Poindexter also was nominated for the annual Ed Block Courage Award, named after former Baltimore Colts trainer Ed Block, the accolade honors players who overcame tremendous obstacles and showed courage and a real love for the game of football.

Tessendorf praised Poindexter's work to get back onto the field in 2000, knowing the long hours and tough times the player experienced.

"Anybody who has had a serious knee injury understands what Anthony went through," the trainer said. "But you've got to put a multiple factor of 10 or 20 for him, maybe 100. Anthony's worked unbelievably hard. He's an amazing young man, and he truly deserves this honor."

But the Ravens had to let Poindexter go following the championship season in a salary cap move when they re-signed fullback Sam Gash. He briefly hooked on with the Cleveland Browns in 2001, but his NFL career was over. He was with the last cuts that summer and eventually made it back to Virginia, where he had finished his college career with 342 career tackles, ninth in school history and first among all Cavalier defensive backs. His 12 interceptions also ranked him fifth in school history.

He's also well remembered for a play that some feel might have been the biggest in school history. Poindexter combined with Adrian Burnim to stiff Florida State running back Warrick Dunn at the goal line as time ran out to help the Wahoos hang on to a 33-28 victory over the Seminoles in 1995.

The victory was that much bigger because Florida State was working on a four-year, 29-game winning streak since coming into the ACC in 1992.

Another Big Mac

The 2003 season might have been the turning point in cornerback Chris McAlister's career.

The speedy and talented defensive back has raised eyebrows throughout his Ravens' career—both for his spectacular plays on the field and his sometimes poor judgment on and off the field.

His 98-yard interception return for a touchdown gave the Ravens the lead for good en route to a 34-20 victory over the New York Jets in the 2000 regular-season finale. He rebounded from a shaky performance against Jacksonville in the season's second game, and by season's end, McAlister was a much more polished defender who helped the team win the Super Bowl.

McAlister eventually became the team's top defensive back as he gained experience and salary cap problems forced Baltimore to let go of other players. But trouble seemed to keep finding him at various times.

He had to deal with a petty theft conviction from 1996 when the Ravens drafted him in the first round of the 1999 draft. He was hit with an unnecessary roughness call that sparked a late Cleveland touchdown drive that helped the Browns pull out an emotional 14-13 victory and eliminate the Ravens from playoff contention in the next to last game of the 2002 season.

McAlister then was arrested during 2003 training camp for driving under the influence. He later was suspended by the team and sat out its win over the Chargers after violating team rules. But the game on the bench seemed to change things. Billick and other teammates made clear their support of McAlister, but also said they wanted him to dedicate himself to being the kind of football player everyone knew he could be.

With each year in the league, Chris McAlister's play has improved.
(Photo by Mitchell Layton)

The cornerback began quietly going about his business and changing himself. McAlister didn't say much to the media for a while, and when he did, the words were much more carefully selected. As the season wore on and the Ravens desperately needed their defense to carry the load, McAlister kept shutting down big receivers.

Plaxico Burress, Chad Johnson, Terrell Owens, Koren Robinson, Chris Chambers, Jimmy Smith—McAlister kept them all quiet in a season in which he finally got his respect. McAlister was then thrilled when he learned of his first Pro Bowl invitation.

"I'm happy, that's all I can say," McAlister said. "I'm very grateful, very blessed. That's basically what it boils down to. It's a great individual accomplishment. That's what it is. It kind of helps to define me."

McAlister and others seemed surprised that he hadn't gotten the honor before this, but the Pro Bowl nod could be a turning point in his career. It's a huge sign of respect and honor.

"It was worth the wait," McAlister said. "I'm excited. I'm happy about it. I got real choked up about it when I found out. The bottom line is that it's something that I've been waiting for."

McAlister made it very clear where he'd like to remain for the rest of his career. The second half of the season was perfect for him and the Ravens. Now they just needed to work out a contract.

"I can definitely see things working out to where I will come back here," McAlister said late in the season. "That's something I'm not worried about, whether I'll be here or not. I honestly believe I will be a Raven."

The Quiet Linebacker

A few days after the 2003 season ended, Peter Boulware quietly limped into a Subway restaurant near the Ravens' training complex to get some lunch. The shop wasn't crowded, and the linebacker placed his order, got his meal and left.

No fanfare, no autographs, no TV lights, no reporters following him. In fact, no one even realized it was him. But that's Peter Boulware.

Boulware has been one of the league's best linebackers since the Ravens drafted him. But he's also been a bit in the shadow of Ray Lewis, the man he's played beside for his whole career. Lewis has received national and international attention for his talents while Boulware, a much quieter personality, just goes about his work.

"I do a little bit of everything," Boulware said. "I blitz a little bit. I cover [and] I'm just kind of all over the field. Wherever they need me to be, I'll be there."

That's been Boulware's mantra since coming to the team as a first-round pick—fourth overall—in the 1997 draft. He came from Florida State with a huge reputation as a great pass rusher. Boulware totaled 32 sacks in his 13 starts for the Seminoles and came out after his junior year.

The Ravens took him in 1997 as they were desperately trying to rebuild a defense that was one of the NFL's worst during their first year in Baltimore. He got off to a quick start, earning Defensive Rookie of the Year honors in 1997, and went on from there.

Boulware had 58 tackles and 8.5 sacks in 2003 and earned his fourth Pro Bowl invite, but his value to the team showed when he was hurt late in the season. He set a team record with an AFC-best 15 sacks in 2001 and now has 67.5 for his Baltimore career.

A knee injury kept him out of the season finale against Pittsburgh and then again sidelined the linebacker in the team's playoff battle with Tennessee. Losing Boulware cost Baltimore a big chunk of its pass rush, and the Ravens weren't able to get the pressure on Tennessee quarterback Steve McNair that's necessary to keep him from moving around and causing trouble.

Boulware has also earned Pro Bowl trips in 1998, 1999, and 2002 and combined with Lewis and others like Jamie Sharper, Edgerton Hartwell and Terrell Suggs to give the Ravens arguably the best linebacking group in the NFL.

But Boulware hasn't gotten quite as much notoriety as Lewis, for a variety of reasons. He's a more low-key personality than Lewis, who doesn't mind dancing out of the tunnel before home games to get the fans fired up. Boulware's locker is right by Lewis's at the team's practice facility, and he'll talk to the media just as much, but he's a bit more serious when talking. You can see it in his face.

Boulware has developed into a solid all-around linebacker since coming to Baltimore. The Ravens were hoping for him to be the sack master (45) that he's become, but Boulware has become even more. He's had to battle through shoulder injury problems earlier in his career and often sees double-teams that make his life tougher on the field.

In the end, the Ravens look at Boulware to give their pass rush an extra boost, and that's what he does—quietly.

"I'll say this—I wouldn't be a competitor unless I wanted to lead the NFL in sacks," Boulware said. "That's what I want to do. I want to be at the top, so every year that's the first goal for an individual pass rusher. But I want to win. If it causes me to sacrifice a few sacks here and there for us to win, that's fine with me."

The Time in the 40 Didn't Matter After All

Terrell Suggs was one of the hot defensive names heading into the 2003 draft. The Arizona State star then saw his name cool off a bit when some teams became alarmed at his slower time in the 40 at postseason workouts heading into the draft.

That reportedly was a reason why he slipped to the No. 10 spot in the first round of the draft, something the Ravens were very happy to see. They picked Suggs and made him a line-backer, and he earned the NFL's Defensive Rookie of the Year award—despite starting only one game.

Suggs wasn't worried about his time in the 40 before the season.

"I wasn't concerned at all," he said in a conference call after the draft. "I thought I was going to be judged to play football, not judged how I was going to do in track speed, but that's what happened, and it happened. I'm a football player, so I'm not really stressing about anything else."

Suggs said from the beginning that he wasn't worried about being drafted at the No. 10 spot. He said at that first press conference that going to play for the Baltimore defense excited him.

"Everybody saw that that defense dominated," Suggs said. "It was the best defense of all time, even better than the Steel Curtain. I was like, 'Wow, what would it be like to play on a defense like that?' And now I get the opportunity to. I'm going to make the most of it, and I'm going to enjoy this."

Suggs started slowly at times in the 2003 season after a brief holdout. The Ravens put him mostly in situations that would let him use his considerable pass-rushing talents, and he went on to get 12 sacks, recover four fumbles and get an interception.

"Every rookie in the NFL knows that it's hard to come into the league and just perform good enough to get an award for it," Suggs said on the team's website. "I'm kind of still overwhelmed by the whole thing. I'm just kind of taking it all in right now. It's a great thing."

Suggs's 24 sacks during his last year at Arizona State set an NCAA mark. He played defensive end there and helped develop the pass-rushing skills that made him so valuable to the Ravens. He quickly found success as a rookie by tying an NFL record with sacks in his first four games and took off from there.

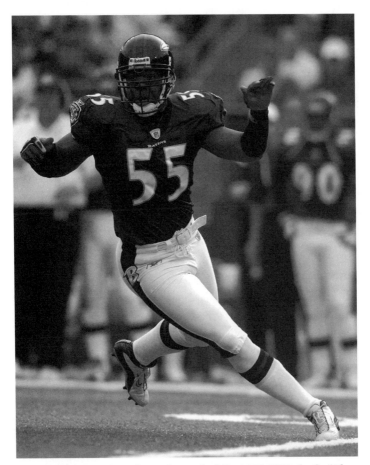

Terrell Suggs may have been the steal of the 2003 NFL draft. (Photo by Mitchell Layton)

Never Giving Up

Marques Douglas wanted to be a defensive lineman in the NFL. But he had a few things going against him—like coming from a small college (Howard) that wasn't exactly a factory for pro players and being a bit small (six foot two, 270 lbs.) himself.

Douglas was a dominant player for some good teams at Howard during his career that ended in 1999—getting 39.5 sacks in 40 starts—but didn't get drafted the following spring. Former Denver defensive back Steve Wilson was Howard's coach at the time and said that Douglas would be a good fit in the NFL.

"He'd fit on the right kind of team," Wilson said then.

Baltimore then signed Douglas to the practice squad, where he spent 14 of the 16 games. Douglas made it to the 53-man roster for two games but was inactive each time. New Orleans then grabbed Douglas off waivers in August of 2000. He finally got a shot to play for the first time in the fourth week before suffering a season-ending knee injury in practice a few days later.

The injury pushed Douglas even harder, as he made it back for training camp with the Saints the following summer but was one of the final cuts. Douglas got a spot on the New Orleans practice squad, where he stayed for the first 11 games of 2001. But then injuries actually gave Douglas a break.

Injuries had crippled the Ravens' defensive line that season at different points, especially towards season's end. Baltimore signed him to the active roster in late November, and Douglas finally got his chance. Douglas showed some promise in two games. He recorded a sack in a shutout of Cincinnati and then received a real shot the following summer (2002), after the Ravens did their salary cap purge.

Douglas became one of the surprises of the season at defensive end. He was having a solid year with 15 tackles and one sack before tearing his ACL in an incident during the Ravens' loss at Indianapolis in their fifth game.

But Douglas didn't lose his cool. Talking in an interview after surgery several days later, Douglas just smiled when asked about if he was disappointed.

"Don't worry," he said. "I'll be back."

And so he was. There were questions about what his role would be with the 2003 Ravens. Some even whispered that he might not make the team. But Douglas looked great in camp and quickly became a starter at right defensive end.

He finished sixth on the team in the regular season with 63 tackles, had four and a half sacks, and got stronger and stronger as the season progressed. Douglas capped it off with a spectacular performance in the season finale, a 13-10 overtime victory over Pittsburgh on national television.

The defensive end was everywhere, getting eight tackles and two and a half sacks as the Ravens shut down the Steelers. He played even better, one of the team leaders in tackles, during Tennessee's 20-17 playoff victory over the Ravens one week later.

Douglas looked like he had turned the clock back to those days at Howard when he battled through double-teams all by himself and racked up 39 quarterback sacks for the Bison.

Douglas had been mainly a first- and second-down player for the Ravens, but with injuries sidelining pass rusher Peter Boulware, the defensive end was called on for more third-down work.

"I just wanted to show that...I can make those plays that sometimes people think I can't make as far as rushing the passer. I've already proved that I can play on first and second team," Douglas said. "I just wanted to put the period at the end of a sentence of a great year."

But Douglas also said it was the period on a chapter of his career. He finally had proved he could be an NFL player for an entire season, one who could really help a team.

And it felt good.

"Now you finally have that chance to start for an NFL season, it's truly a blessing," Douglas said. "All year, you want to make those bigger plays, you want to be counted as one of those core guys that the Ravens look to that when times get tight, you're going to come through for them, and I just think that [against Pittsburgh], I was in a zone."

The one question Douglas did have to answer was about the unusual dance he did after one of his sacks.

"I'm going to work on that," Douglas said with a little laugh. "Maybe I'll shy away from dancing a little bit."

"The Buddy Lee Group"

Douglas was part of one of the most surprising groups of the 2002 and 2003 seasons—one that Billick and others called the "Buddy Lee group."

The Ravens switched to a 3-4 format after losing Adams, Burnett and Siragusa following the 2001 season when the team had to go through a salary purge. They knew that McCrary would be back, but knee injuries eventually stopped him. So the Ravens had to gamble on an untested group of starters for the 2003 season.

That left second-round draft pick Anthony Weaver, a rookie from Notre Dame, along with Douglas and nose tackle Kelly Gregg, to form the starting defensive line. Billick and others eventually coined the phrase the "Buddy Lee group" to describe what the coach called a "a group that not many had heard of."

Weaver was somewhat known because he was a high draft pick. But he had just one year's experience. Douglas was probably the player almost no one had heard of since Howard played Division I-AA football. But he became not just a solid player but a starter. Gregg also came from just as far out of nowhere.

He was a solid player for Oklahoma in college. The six-foot, 310-pound Gregg really went down a tough road. The Bengals picked him in the sixth round of the 1999 draft. Cincinnati waived him on September 6, 1999 and then signed him to the practice squad two days later.

Philadelphia then signed him on December 8 before waiving him on September 12, 2000. The Ravens signed Gregg the following day, and he spent the season on the practice squad. Gregg then was signed to the active roster in February, 2001.

Gregg was one of the many players who people felt simply wouldn't be either good enough or ready to play at this level. But he surprised people right from the start when finally seeing action.

In 2001, Gregg was inactive for the season's first four games before getting in for three plays during the team's loss at Green Bay. Gregg then sat for three more games before the Ravens' mounting injuries opened the door.

Gregg got in for 17 plays in Cleveland's surprising win over the Ravens on November 18—and made people take notice with four tackles, including his first career sack. He began seeing more and more action throughout the season and finished with 19 tackles, the sack and one pass defended.

Gregg and Douglas represented two of the team's biggest questions heading into 2003. Could the smallish Gregg make it through a full season at nose tackle, taking the pounding that that position requires? And could Douglas stay away from injuries long enough?

Douglas did just fine, and Gregg turned out to be better than anyone dreamed. He finished the regular season ranked fourth on the team in tackles. Then at season's end, the Ravens ended his long journey by signing him to a five-year contract with, according to *The Baltimore Sun*, a $2 million signing bonus.

"That's what it's all about, getting an opportunity in this league and trying to take advantage of it," Gregg said a few days after signing the contract. "Just work hard and keep working."

Gregg said that, even when on the practice squad, he felt he had a shot at doing something with the Ravens.

"I knew that...the Baltimore Ravens would give me a chance," Gregg said. "Here they let people compete for anywhere."

A Quiet Leader

Bringing in Shannon Sharpe proved a key move for the Ravens before the 2000 season as the veteran quickly stepped in as a vocal leader on the team. But Sharpe wasn't the only veteran free agent who is likely headed for the Hall of Fame.

The Ravens had signed veteran defensive back Rod Woodson two years earlier, and he helped stabilize a young backfield. Woodson's leadership played a big role in aiding young defensive backs like Chris McAlister and Duane Starks throughout the championship season in 2000.

Woodson was considered one of the greatest cornerbacks ever to play in the NFL during his 10 years with the Pittsburgh Steelers (1987-1996). A knee injury slowed him during Pittsburgh's Super Bowl season, and after a year with San Francisco, he came to Baltimore in 1998 as a starter at safety.

Woodson had little trouble making the move and simply became a very tough safety instead of being angry over not playing cornerback.

"It's definitely a different challenge," Woodson said during the 2001 season. "Corners and safeties are different. Corners are on an island, and at safety you're controlling a lot of things from different angles."

Woodson's experience made Billick very happy with the move and not worried at all about putting the veteran in a new position.

"What situation has Rod Woodson not been in or seen?" Billick asked. "And he passes that on to the other guys."

Woodson admittedly had lost a step, probably a combination of the knee problems and age, but most still felt he could play at cornerback. But while he was with the Ravens, youngsters McAlister and Starks were handling that job and learning from him.

"For a young guy looking up and seeing what type of player he is on the field and off the field, he's an inspiration," Starks said during the 2001 season. "He's a leader to the [younger guys]. He's helped me and helped Chris."

Woodson was a member of the NFL's 75th Anniversary Team and moved on to Oakland after the 2001 season. He started for the Raiders again in 2002 and 2003 and showed the same ability he displayed with the Ravens.

The Versatility Factor

The Baltimore Ravens really liked the athleticism of Adalius Thomas when they picked him in the sixth round of the 2000 draft. But it's doubtful they realized exactly how much of an athlete they were getting.

Thomas came from Southern Mississippi, where he was twice named the Conference USA Defensive Player of the Year, and the Ravens saw the six-foot-two, 270-pound athlete as a linebacker and/or defensive end.

That's exactly what happened, as Thomas eventually developed into a solid player who helped at both positions along with being a huge force on special teams, being picked for the 2004 Pro Bowl in that position. However, a late-season fractured elbow put Thomas on the injured reserve, kept him out of the Pro Bowl and hurt the Ravens' defense.

The versatility that Thomas brings to the Ravens helps the defense in many ways. He's got speed, quickness and power. Thomas is a strong pass rusher who can easily drop back and cover receivers while also intercepting passes and using his great speed to return them. His great speed also lets him race downfield to help make tackles on the punting team—an unusual combination all the way around.

"We're trying to use his talents," Baltimore defensive coordinator Mike Nolan said during the season. "If we didn't have a guy like him, we wouldn't be using some of the things we're doing. He's a defensive lineman slash linebacker and vice versa. You can call him the 'Defensive Slash.'"

Another slash can be added when talking about his ability to help on the special teams. The Ravens often used him as their "gunner" on special teams. For example, when they punted, the Ravens would line Thomas up outside like a wide receiver and let him race downfield to be one of the first players to have a shot at tackling the punt returner.

"As a gunner, it shows his ability to change direction and still make a play on a small guy," said special teams coach Gary Zauner.

The Ravens needed Thomas to fill some holes during the 2002 season when Ray Lewis missed much of the year with a shoulder injury. The team already had been counting on him to step up because the salary cap problem had forced the team to lose so many players from the playoff teams of 2000 and 2001.

Thomas filled in perfectly, coming up with a career-high 68 tackles plus three sacks. He also had two interceptions—including one he returned for a touchdown against Cincinnati.

Thomas truly showed his versatility during the game in which he was hurt late in the 2003 season. He had five tackles plus two sacks and a forced fumble before breaking his right elbow while trying to recover a fumble.

A free agent after the 2003 season, Thomas was a player the Ravens definitely wanted to try to bring back—simply because he can do so many things.

"Playing linebacker gives me a chance to make more plays," Thomas said. "As an end...I'm not bad at it, but it doesn't fit my athleticism as well as outside linebacker does. I think they are just trying to get the best 11 on the field."

And Thomas usually has been one of them.

Who Is Edgerton Hartwell?

Very few people outside the Ravens even knew who linebacker Edgerton Hartwell was before the 2002 season.

The Ravens picked Hartwell in the fourth round of the 2001 draft, and he saw mostly special teams action that year because Baltimore had many starters back from its Super Bowl championship team of the year before.

But when salary cap problems caused the team to lose a load of starters after the 2001 season, Hartwell received an opportunity to play. And then when star linebacker Ray Lewis injured his shoulder early in the 2002 season and missed most of the rest of the year, Hartwell stepped up in a huge way.

Hartwell led the team with 161 tackles and earned the respect of many throughout the NFL with his tough play. He ended the season with a bang by getting 17 tackles and a sack in the season finale, a 34-31 loss at Pittsburgh.

Hartwell posted some huge numbers after Lewis's injury. He had 16 tackles in a win at Cincinnati and often finished in double figures with tackles.

The play of Edgerton Hartwell has helped to keep the Ravens' defense an elite unit in spite of the loss of many key players. (Photo by Mitchell Layton)

"I think that Edgerton represents the best of the Ravens," Billick said. "He was a guy that knew he was going to have to step up and expand his role, not only physically but also in terms of leadership and making the calls. He stepped up to the challenge and embraced it. He wasn't afraid of the challenge."

The linebacker definitely agreed with Billick, especially when it came to his goals in each game.

"My goals aren't real complicated," Hartwell said. "I want to be a football player, a great linebacker and a gladiator for the

Baltimore Ravens. I want to beat you up, get in your head and settle it man to man. If you don't want to be great you're cheating your team."

Now with Lewis, Boulware, and others, the Ravens have a solid group of linebackers who won't cheat the team in any way.

Matte's Musings on Ed Hartwell

"Let me tell you one thing—what a tough football player he is, what a great attitude. Here's another guy who will just do anything to win. He's just humble pie. There's no cockiness about him. He just walks around with a presence. And last year, what a job he had to step into when Ray Lewis got hurt. How do you even think about doing that? You get your opportunities in life, and you don't get them very often, so you have to take advantage of them. If you're an athlete, and you're an Ed Hartwell or a Tom Matte, what you want to do is when you get a chance to show your wares out there."

A Very Sharp Linebacker

Every team lost someone to the Houston Texans in the 2002 expansion draft, but losing linebacker Jamie Sharper truly hurt the Ravens, because it broke up one of the best linebacking trios in NFL history.

Sharper, Lewis and Boulware had been together for five seasons and were an integral part of the record-setting 2000 defense that carried the Ravens to a Super Bowl title. Sharper and Boulware were the outside linebackers around middle linebacker Lewis in the 4-3 scheme the Ravens used then.

Boulware and Lewis were both first-round picks (1997 and 1996, respectively) while Sharper was a second-round pick in 1997 out of Virginia and didn't get quite as much notice as the other two. He struggled a bit early on but developed as time went on and always found a way to make plays. He became one of the team's leading tacklers.

Sharper slowly came on and had big seasons for the Ravens in 2000 and 2001. In fact, he was one of the team's top defensive players during its 4-0 postseason run in 2000. He finished with 20 tackles, two sacks and two interceptions during the playoffs.

He also had three tackles, plus one on special teams, along with a big interception in the second quarter of the 34-7 victory over the New York Giants in the Super Bowl, a pick that came while the game was still close.

Sharper fared even better in 2001, knowing it was likely his last year on the team. He developed into a top linebacker, finishing second to Lewis in tackles.

He had 135 tackles during the 2001 season and was a key player. Houston took him in the 2002 expansion draft, and the Texans began building their defense around his talents. The Ravens were able to replace him with Ed Hartwell and others like Terrell Suggs, but the Lewis-Boulware-Sharper linebacking trio was one of the best in NFL history.

The Goose

Tony Siragusa became one of the most popular players in Ravens history. Many Baltimore football fans saw him as a second Artie Donovan, the Hall of Fame defensive lineman who played for the Baltimore Colts in the 1950s and '60s.

The similarities were amazing. Both were very big, very good, and very funny. Donovan and Siragusa both had rather blunt and simple nicknames. Donavan's teammates called him Fatso. Siragusa's nickname was just the Goose.

And everyone loved both of them, but Siragusa turned out to be one of the pieces that turned the Ravens' defense into something special when he came to the team. His huge bulk up front—six foot three, 340 pounds—helped the Ravens. And when Sam Adams joined the team, the pair combined to collapse many offensive lines. The strong play of defensive ends Rob Burnett and McCrary combined with Adams and the Goose in the middle simply let the Baltimore linebackers run wild.

The Goose shows off the latest dance steps after recording a sack. (Photo by Phil Hoffmann)

The fans loved watching the Goose. Siragusa announced late in the 2001 season that he would be retiring, and in his final home game he took a moment to say goodbye in his own style.

Siragusa's picture appeared on the giant screens at the team's stadium during the final minutes of the Ravens' playoff-clinching 19-3 victory over Minnesota. The colorful defensive tackle then thanked the fans by blowing kisses to the crowd, making many laugh on a brutally cold Monday night.

Siragusa had beaten the odds before during an NFL career that began in 1990, when he made the Indianapolis Colts' roster as an undrafted free agent. In 1997, he signed with Baltimore and quickly became an anchor of the defense that carried the Ravens to their Super Bowl championship.

Injuries took their toll on Siragusa and that defense in 2001 after Baltimore suffered few injuries during their Super Bowl in 2000. He underwent minor knee surgery during training camp and missed some other time because of a leg injury.

The media loved the Goose because of, well, his big mouth. Goose wanted to be a media star, and he certainly got his wish. He wanted to go into broadcasting and movies and achieved both goals, recently appearing in a Spike Lee movie and working on a FOX TV sports show.

Goose knew how to work the media. He was a master at saying things that would make it into print or on TV.

For example, when the Ravens' defense was shutting down the league in 2000, people were trying to come up with some kind of nickname for it, like Los Angeles' Fearsome Foursome or Pittsburgh's Steel Curtain. The Purple People Eaters had been taken by the Vikings many years before, but Siragusa simply snorted when asked the question.

"A name for our defense?" the Goose said. "How about 'the best?'"

The Goose also was clever in drawing attention to himself. When he warmed up before the Super Bowl—and then afterwards—many in the media noticed the T-shirt he wore. It was a

Mickey Mouse shirt; some jokingly thought he was trying to get people's attention in order to win the game's MVP award and thus be featured in the famous commercial that goes along with it—a national piece that says something like, hey, Tony Siragusa, you just won the Super Bowl, what are you going to do now? The player then screams that he's going to Disney World. Some thought wearing the T-shirt was Goose's way of getting the Disney folks to notice him. It would be classic Goose.

He played a solid game and the Ravens won easily that day, routing the Giants, 34-7. Goose didn't get the MVP honor, but he sure had a lot of fun.

That was always what the Goose was about, having fun. He always laughed and joked about himself and anything that meant anything to him.

The Goose Goes Hollywood

Let's let Tony Siragusa tell his own story about what it was like to be in a Spike Lee movie. Siragusa told the tale to the Baltimore media when answering questions about what it was like to be coming back to do color on the Ravens' preseason games.

Siragusa started by describing what it was like to get a call from Lee: "It was a squeaky voice. 'This is Spike, Goose.' I said, 'This isn't Spike.' I thought it was one of my buddies, so I hung up on him. He actually called me back and said, 'No, this is really Spike. I want you to be in my movie.' So I questioned him and it was Spike. He said, 'I'm doing this movie and there's an Italian role I want you to play.' So I told him to call my agent and arrange it. So Jimmy, my agent, calls me up, from William Morris, and he says we're going to have a meeting with Spike and to come on in. I sit down with Spike. He invites me to a Knicks-Nets game, so we go. We're hitting it off pretty good.

"He tells me, 'Yeah, it's pretty easy. You can do this.' We didn't talk any about the role for the three meetings we had. All he wanted to talk about was, 'What did the Ravens do before the game? What was it like winning the Super Bowl?' All he wanted to talk about was sports. So I figured that I was doing this Italian role, I'll get it. I'll hang out with my uncles for a little while. I can pick this role up. So he calls me up and says, 'Oh, by the way, it's going to be a Russian role. We've changed your role.' I said, 'You're kidding me, right?'

"So he sends me to this Russian dialect person twice for like an hour, and the next thing you know, we're rolling the scene. I met up with Ed Norton, and I said, 'Listen. If my Russian accent's really bad, let me know.' He said, 'No, no. It sounded good.'

"It was an experience. Going from football right into the acting thing was very, very different. I remember the first day, we had a reading. Everyone came in for a reading and we were sitting down. I was sitting in the corner, thinking that everyone was going to be all artsy. I was just laying low.

"I had my script, because it was a read-through. So we start reading. They pass out another paper on what days you're going to be filming. So this girl's sitting next to me and she's all dressed in black. She looks kind of weird to me. I didn't want to talk to her that much. So I said, 'Let me ask you this. What does this mean? This little P and these other letters and dates?' She said, 'This is when you start, this is when you finish, this is when you come back.' She goes, 'Oh, is this your first role?' And I say, 'Yeah, why? Do I look bad? Do I look like a rookie here?' I was really embarrassed. So I wait a couple of minutes and I look around and I say, 'Is this your first time?' And she goes, 'No, I've done this a few times.' Next thing you know, it's Anna Paquin, who's won an Academy Award, sitting right next to me. That brought me down to earth, I guess. It was fun."

That's much better than we could have done. Good luck in the movies, Goose.

Matte's Musings on the Goose

"The Goose is a legend all by himself. Just ask him, he'll tell you. I think every team has to have a player like him to keep everybody loose. The Goose and Artie Donovan, what a comparison. I had a chance to play with Artie for a couple of years, and I'll tell you one thing, he kept everybody light. The Goose was the same way, but when the game day came, the Goose put up. He shut up and he put up. He came out there and played good football, good solid football. They kept alternating other guys in there like Larry Webster and Lional Dalton, and they did a great job. It kept everyone fresh.

"With Goose and Sam Adams up front, they gave Ray Lewis and the linebackers a lot of leeway as far as what they wanted to do. They would tie up the middle, and they'd do the bull-rush in there. The Goose really did remind me of Artie Donovan. Watch the screen. Watch the draw. The fans just loved him. They loved him. He had a great personality, and he also had the ability. He really was a good football player. He would make light of everything. You have to have somebody around who loosens up the team. He made everybody laugh, and everybody had a good time. I always had fun when I played. I would always be a joker, and the Goose was always like that. You have to have someone like that. He was the class clown. I think that brought that team a lot closer together. With the leadership they had and the coaching staff they had, it was a good thing. The Goose was just great because he'd come off the wall with something. You just never knew what he was going to do."

The Growth of Gary Baxter

The Ravens relied heavily on a very strong secondary during their Super Bowl run in 2000 and making the playoffs the following season. But they lost starters Rod Woodson, Duane Starks, Kim Herring and other valuable players to free agency and the salary cap purge and needed some help from younger players to rebuild.

Baltimore slowly began to reshape its secondary with strong performances from younger players. Ed Reed became a star almost immediately and made the Pro Bowl in his second year. McAlister shook off some problems and finally made the Pro Bowl, also like Reed for the first time in 2003.

But the Ravens weren't quite sure what to do with Gary Baxter after picking him in the second round of the 2001 draft. A training camp knee injury shelved him for the first eight games of that season, and he saw some action at times on special teams and from scrimmage in six games.

Baxter showed the Ravens he could play at both cornerback and safety, and they shifted him between the spots before eventually making him the starter at corner.

Baxter said he didn't really mind switching between the two positions.

"For me, it's more of a challenge," he said. "I think I play better when I'm under a lot of pressure. I tend to respond. Going from safety to nickel to corner, I've been doing it so much, it's starting to be normal for me. It's not easy, but it's something I really like to do."

Baxter locked up his starting spot at cornerback in 2003, tying Kelly Gregg for third on the team with 87 tackles. He also had three interceptions and worked with McAlister at shutting down many receivers as teams often threw against the Ravens, who were one of the NFL's best teams against the run.

But Baxter's versatility simply gives the Ravens more options in every game.

"We never imagined that he would be able to [play both corner and safety] at this level as well as he is," said Baltimore's assistant director of pro personnel, Vince Newsome. "No one in the league does it."

Another Comeback Story

Cornell Brown came to the Ravens as a sixth-round pick in the 1997 draft. The linebacker from Virginia Tech helped the team almost immediately.

Brown made plays on special teams and at linebacker for the young and growing defense. He had 25 tackles plus a career-best three sacks and caused two fumbles during the Super Bowl championship season in 2000.

But everything fell apart after that. Brown was hit with a drug charge in 2001, and the Ravens waived him on September, 5. He dropped out of football that year but didn't just sit around staring at the walls; he went back to Virginia Tech to complete his degree in consumer studies.

The charge was eventually dropped, but the Ravens noticed and liked how Brown worked at getting his life back together. After Oakland signed and then released Brown before the 2002 season, the Ravens picked him back up. Baltimore re-signed him on August 20, and Brown jumped right back in.

He started 14 of the 16 games, helping in a huge way when Ray Lewis went down for the season with a shoulder injury. Brown finished with a career-high 67 tackles and added 1.5 sacks.

"In the off season, I saw the young man went back and got his degree," Billick said. "That tells me something. The NFL keeps preaching to the players to overcome your mistakes, get your degree, go back to school. When a young man does that, it tells you something. To me, that says Cornell learned some life lessons and deserves that other spot."

Brown didn't see as much playing time in 2003 because the injuries were fewer and farther between with rookie Terrell Suggs becoming more of an influence. But the veteran still pitched in with 33 tackles and one sack, and the Ravens are glad to have him back.

Another Find from Out of the Blue

The Ravens were looking for help from all kinds of places heading into the 2002 season. The well documented salary cap purge forced the team to get rid of or lose numerous key players, especially in the secondary.

Baltimore knew it would have to ask younger players like McAlister, Baxter, Reed and others to step up in a big way, and they did. But free agent Will Demps turned out to be one of the biggest surprises in franchise history.

The six-foot, 205-pound safety from San Diego State joined the Ravens and worked his way into the starting lineup, an even more impressive feat given the fact that he needed to recover from a dislocated elbow suffered in the preseason.

That injury sidelined Demps the first two games, but he bounced back to start 10 of the 14 games he appeared in and just kept finding ways to make plays. Demps made only one interception all year—but it came with three seconds left on the Baltimore goal line and clinched the October 20 win over Jacksonville.

He began with a rush, making eight tackles in his career debut when the Ravens shocked Denver on a Monday night game in Baltimore. Demps struggled at times but kept bouncing back to make big plays.

Demps did the same thing in 2003. He started nine games and played in all 16 games and had two interceptions while playing a major role in the secondary. But in the end, he just kept finding ways to make big plays.

"A lot of things were thrown at me that first year," Demps said. "I got hurt, the confidence and hitting that [rookie] wall. I took that all off season, saw what I did wrong, and now I just have more confidence."

The confidence paid off as Demps became a solid player for Baltimore, and the Ravens are hoping he keeps improving.

"A lot of people thought I was a one-year wonder, but I don't want that," Demps said. "I'm going to contribute any-where they need me, on special teams, wherever."

Matte's Musings on Ed Reed

"Ed Reed, to me, is probably the most complete safety I've seen in so long that it's unbelievable. He just has a complete sense of what the game is all about. For a second-year guy, it's unbeliev-able how he reads the quarterback, how he looks at the pass pat-tern developing, how he sets up that quarterback to throw that ball and break on it. He's way beyond his years. I've talked to Billick about him. He had the maturity as a sophomore to be the captain at Miami. He came here, and this guy, I'll tell you, he's something. I've talked to other guys, and he's great. The way he sets these guys up on punt blocks is unbelievable. He'll block the punt and then he has the presence to pick the ball up and run it in. He's in a class by himself. The kid comes through for them, he leads by example, and I think there's a lot of respect for him on defense."

Chapter 7

JAMAL LEWIS

What a Rush

Some people wondered if the Baltimore Ravens were making a mistake when they took Jamal Lewis in the first round of the 2000 draft. The five-foot-eleven, 231-pound Lewis was obviously a powerful runner, having posted some big numbers at Tennessee, but he had suffered a serious knee injury that raised some questions.

Could he stay healthy? Would he be a workhorse back? Those were the questions many had when the Ravens picked Lewis with the fifth overall selection in 2000. And he answered several of those queries immediately by rushing for a franchise-record 1,364 yards that season while helping the Ravens to a Super Bowl title.

But those questions came up again when Lewis suffered a knee injury in training camp that ended his 2001 season before it started. Lewis then bounced back for a strong 2002 season, rushing for 1,327 yards and showing he was back.

Jamal Lewis hits the hole, ready to make a big run for the Ravens in the Super Bowl. (Photo by Phil Hoffmann)

The question then was what would he do in 2003. Lewis rededicated himself to tough training in the off season, coming into camp in tip-top shape and staying that way throughout the season. That's a big reason why he rushed for an NFL-best 2,066 yards. It was the second best single-season effort of any rusher in history, behind only Eric Dickerson's 2,105-yard effort in 1984, and earned Lewis the NFL's Offensive Player of the Year award.

"I don't count how many carries I get, and I don't keep track of the yards," Lewis said. "I know how many yards I have because someone in the media is always telling me. I just put one foot in front of the other and let the yards add up, hopefully, to help win games."

Lewis wound up facing national attention for much of the season, but he handled it well. He often had large crowds of media members in front of his practice locker during the week, but he answered all the questions quietly and with little fanfare.

"I don't care about the attention," Lewis said. "It's all right. I'm a shy guy. I just take it as it comes."

The jumping-off point came with Lewis's spectacular effort against Cleveland in the season's second game. Lewis ran for an NFL-record 295 yards on 30 carries to give the Ravens a 33-13 win over the Browns in Baltimore.

That game drew national attention and put Lewis under a spotlight that he stayed in throughout the year. He took over the NFL lead in rushing, stayed there the rest of the season and went into the season's final game—against Pittsburgh—with a shot at breaking Dickerson's record.

Adding to the pressure in that game was that it was ESPN's *Sunday Night Football* telecast, and the network naturally had Dickerson sitting at his house watching the telecast and joking around. Making it even more interesting was the fact that Cincinnati already had lost earlier in the afternoon, clinching the AFC North title for the Ravens.

That put Billick in an interesting situation. Should he leave his top offensive player out there to go for a record or hold him to get ready for the playoffs later in the week?

Billick had insisted early in the week that he would treat it like a normal game—and he did just that. Lewis got 73 yards early, but the Steelers stacked up their defense and refused to let the record be broken on their watch. He finished with 114 yards that night.

Still, the Ravens—especially the offensive line—took great pride in Lewis's accomplishments. They loved it when he broke the single-game record against Cleveland, which started the whole big season.

"It was spectacular to be part of this," Ogden said. "For offensive linemen, this is the best—it was beautiful to see. Man, to be 240 pounds and that fast. Beautiful, just beautiful."

The Tennessee Titans also concentrated hard on stopping Lewis in the first-round playoff game. They stacked the line like the Steelers did and limited him to just 35 yards on only 14 carries—a season low in a game where Lewis really wasn't much of a factor—as the Titans eliminated the Ravens with a 20-17 victory.

Tennessee pushed up to nine players on the line and did a great job of taking away the running game (specifically Lewis) that the Ravens had relied upon all season long. The Titans clogged the running lanes and made moving the ball on the ground nearly impossible.

So the Ravens, ranked last in the NFL in passing, had to throw. Anthony Wright did well at times, but showed how much they relied on Lewis. Billick took some heat for only giving Lewis the ball 14 times, but the coach said he didn't have much choice.

"They committed their resources to stop the run, and they did a great job," said Billick the day after the game. "I mean, they were set to stop the ball and we made some plays outside—obviously not enough. The young man ran for over 2,000 yards. I think we handed the ball off enough to him."

In 2003, Jamal Lewis set the single-game rushing record, and came oh-so-close to breaking the season rushing record. (Photo by Mitchell Layton)

"It Was Awesome to Watch"

Lewis was well known for his abilities before the season began, but he truly impressed many with his work. Here's what some others said about what he did in 2003, especially the 295-yard game against Cleveland.

ESPN commentator Joe Theismann: "There's no doubt Jamal Lewis is one of the top three running backs in the NFL. He's up there with Clinton Portis and Priest Holmes in terms of all-around excellence. I don't care who you run for 295 yards against, whether it be a college or even a high school team. That's a great performance by a great player. It's amazing that a player who has rushed for over 1,300 yards in his two seasons is underrated...he's a huge reason why the Ravens won the Super Bowl in his rookie season."

New York Giants running back Tiki Barber: "As an NFL fan, it was exciting to watch Jamal Lewis break the all-time single-game rushing record. As an NFL running back, it was awesome to watch. To accomplish what Jamal did is simply incredible to me. What's even more impressive to me is that he is two seasons removed from major knee surgery."

Cincinnati LB Kevin Hardy: "Jamal's the kind of running back where, if you let him get rolling and he gets his pads down, he can just rip your arms out of the sockets. He's a big guy with power, but he's got some speed, too. Plus, he's shifty. When he has momentum, and he's running downhill, look out. Man, he's tough to tackle."

Ravens LB Ray Lewis: "He has the same energy as me, but he wouldn't display it. I'd tell him to show the offense that side of himself because they would see him as a leader. He's learning he shouldn't hide his charisma. His teammates need that."

The Teacher

Jamal Lewis was a huge part of the Ravens' offense in 2000. Baltimore loved his rarely seen mix of speed and power. Simply put, he could run over you or run through you. Lewis came up

Priest Holmes served as a mentor and teacher to Jamal Lewis during Lewis's rookie year. Now, both are racking up impressive numbers every Sunday. (Photo by Phil Hoffmann)

big in his rookie year, and he gave many thanks to a quiet and classy running back named Priest Holmes.

Holmes had 1,008 yards for Baltimore in 1998 and showed himself to be a multitalented guy who also could catch passes. The Ravens, however, liked Lewis and thought he might be better for the type of offense they ran. They told Holmes during Lewis's rookie year in 2000 that he'd be used more as a third-down type of back.

Holmes knew that and didn't pout like many would. Instead he worked hard at teaching the rookie the ropes. He took Lewis under his wing and showed him about NFL life. Lewis said he'll always be grateful for the way Holmes behaved—although the rookie did have to buy the food for the informal film sessions they'd have at night.

"I kind of followed in his path," Lewis said. "I kind of called him my mentor. He taught me a lot of things that really paved the way."

Billick said that the Ravens would have loved to keep both backs, but Holmes wanted to be a starter somewhere. Baltimore simply couldn't pay two running backs the big money.

"There's such a fondness for Priest from this organization," Billick said. "You can't help but feel good for Priest for the success he's had."

Holmes signed with Kansas City and gained 1,555 yards the first year (2001) and led the NFL in 2002 with 2,287 total yards from scrimmage—the fourth highest total in league history. Holmes won the NFL rushing title that year and was voted the Associated Press' Offensive Player of the Year in 2002. He gained over 2,000 yards of total offense in 2003.

Many people know what Priest Holmes has done in Kansas City. But the quiet things he did with a rookie running back in Baltimore in 2000 that count among his most valuable acts.

Matte's Musings on Jamal Lewis and Other Offensive Questions

"He was suspect when he first came in, as far as I was concerned, because of the knee. I thought that from the surgery he had, it was so severe, people wondered if he could come back. Could he come back and show up? He's 240 pounds. The last five, six or seven years I played, I weighed about 220-225, and my offensive line averaged about 245. Our offensive line now is about 330 pounds. All these guys have to do is give him a seam. This guy is in the superstar category right now. He should be up there with the Jim Browns because that's how good I think he can be. And I thought Jim Brown was the probably the biggest, strongest running back who ever played the game. Jamal just wants to do his job on the field.

"That's another reason why I like him so much. He's got a great mental attitude toward the game. He prepares himself and he wants the ball. Get me the ball any way you can get me the ball. He makes that clear to Billick. And they get him the ball. It's a lot of work, and he took some shots this year. This is where Billick is smart. He put in guys like Chester Taylor and Musa Smith. Jamal knows that Billick is looking for him.

"The thing that I'm so impressed about with Jamal is that he's come back after having two [major] operations on his knees. They were both reconstructed. I think he's one of the most disciplined athletes that I've ever known. I have been absolutely taken aback by the way he is. He's such a quiet kid. He's a shy kid. There's no cockiness about him at all. He's the ultimate football player. That's all. Do you see that he hands the ball to the official after scoring a touchdown or making a play? I'm totally impressed with him. He could have played with us on the Colts back when I played. He reminds me a lot of Jim Taylor of the Packers and also someone like Gale Sayers. You never heard

Jim shooting his mouth off. He enjoyed the game. He really enjoyed it.

"Jamal is such an exceptional athlete, to be able to handle the endurance of a whole 20-game season. Billick has got to be given some credit for that also, because of the way he handled it. I think the coaches sometimes lose perspective with running backs. I can tell you that from experience. You really get beat up, and your butt is handed to you. If you take a look at a running back's body, you can see. That's management and is a key integral part of keeping a running back healthy. That's where coaching comes in. Coaches have got to know and feel what a player can do. They have to have a pulse of that team and the pulse of each player, because if you burn them out, then what the hell good is it?

"To me, Jamal Lewis is a disciplined athlete. He works continually in the off season and is in tremendous condition because it's become a full-time job for him. Because of his knees, to be able to come back is really something special. But Jamal finally figured out after a couple of years what it took to stay healthy for a whole year. I think working out with Ray Lewis on a regular basis was a key.

"Ray pushes you to the next level. That's where leadership comes in. On Jamal's 295-yard game, the offensive line rose to the occasion. You can stop Jamal five times in a row, but that sixth time he's going to break it. Once he got past those linebackers, he was in the secondary, [and] with his speed and his power, he is very tough to stop. Whenever you take the chance of doing the eight and nine guys in box defense, if Jamal breaks through that seam, he's off to the races.

"But in terms of the offense overall, when that happens you've got to be able to go to your receivers. Let's say you've got one-on-one coverage and you've got to get open. You use a play-action to hold them for a while, and the Ravens didn't do that much this season.

"The offensive line never gets the credit for success like Jamal had this year, but Jamal went right to the offensive line and said thanks. You can never do it on your own. The receivers did a good job of going and getting in the way. When you're a running back, all the wide receivers have to do is get down and get in the way. That's the amazing part of it. No matter how many people they had up there, the Ravens were still able to establish the running game. The offensive line had to do a hell of a job, and Jamal ran some people over. Jamal is just a tremendously conditioned athlete.

"I think there'll be some pressure put on him. He made it to the Pro Bowl this year, which he should have with what he did. He now has to keep himself at the same level. It's imperative that he understands that a running game establishes a passing game. If the Ravens can get a passing game together, it will be a hell of a combination. There's no question about it. They're looking at last year, and they'll run the ball down our throat or we have to drop back and play the pass. That makes the running game more effective. If I'm playing defense against Baltimore, I'm praying to God that they don't get a passing game going. They have to somehow improve that passing game.

"I think that with the draft and the free agent market, they ought to be really looking around to find someone to step up and do what they need. My estimation is that the Ravens need one or two receivers and a couple of offensive linemen who they can bring along."

Chapter 8

THE OFFENSE

The Baby

Jermaine Lewis and his wife, Imara, received a horrible shock when their long-awaited son was stillborn on December 13, 2000. That was on a Wednesday. The Ravens were set to leave a few days later for a game in Arizona with the Cardinals, and Billick didn't hesitate.

He called Lewis and told him to forget about the Cardinals. The Ravens put Lewis on the inactive list for that game. "You need to be with your wife," Billick said. The Ravens were quiet about why Lewis wasn't playing, saying it was a personal matter.

But when the word began to trickle out, an amazing rush of sympathy followed for Lewis. The wide receiver had been popular in Baltimore since his rookie year in 1996. Lewis grew up in nearby Prince George's County and was a star in high school football and track and then went on to become an offensive force with Maryland.

Jermaine Lewis overcame family tragedy to score the decisive touch-down in Super Bowl XXXV. (Photo by Phil Hoffmann)

The Ravens took him in the fifth round of the 1996 draft. Lewis wanted desperately to be a multitalented guy, a wide receiver/kick returner who made opponents sweat. And he could often do just that, epecially with his exciting kick returns.

However, Lewis's size left people in the Ravens' organization wondering if he was big enough to handle the demands of being a receiver. Lewis was only five foot seven and 180 pounds, and he often took some brutal hits, especially when he would line up in the slot.

Billick and his staff felt he was too valuable as a punt returner—and occasional kickoff returner—to risk. But Lewis's ability to make the big plays endeared him to the Baltimore faithful. And when he returned after taking the week off to mourn the loss of his son, Lewis did something that touched the hearts of many.

The Ravens' offense had a shaky day against the New York Jets, but the play of Lewis helped Baltimore pull out a wild 34-20 victory on a cold and windy day. He returned two punts for touchdowns and pointed to the sky each time while racing to the end zone, basically telling his son Geronimo that this was for him.

Lewis caught national attention a few weeks later when his 84-yard kickoff return for a touchdown broke open the Super Bowl moments after the Giants had scored. In a photo of the moment that became very popular in Baltimore, Lewis is running all alone, a few steps from the end zone, with the ball in his left hand and pointing to the sky with his right.

The Leader

The Ravens made no bones about why they signed Shannon Sharpe before the 2000 season. They wanted a leader who could help a team on the verge of becoming a winner become one.

Sharpe was a leader from the moment he signed with the Ravens. The talkative tight end quietly took Ray Lewis under his wing, showed him what it meant to be a leader, and was a big reason why the linebacker became such a presence with the Ravens.

Sharpe was in Atlanta during Lewis's highly publicized trial and worked out with him at the gym on a regular basis, helping take his mind off the situation he was facing.

"Shannon has been a person who literally pulled me through this," Lewis said at his press conference when he returned to Baltimore after the trial ended. "I mean, I was leaving court, and from court I was going to work out. I mean, he didn't even give me 30 minutes to sit down and harp on it."

Sharpe spent two seasons with the Ravens and truly became a leader. He had been through it all with Denver and wasn't afraid to deal with the media and the pressure.

"You can't quantify what a Shannon Sharpe does for your team," Billick said after the season. "He is a winner. He has won three of the last four Super Bowls. He has an aura, a presence and it is apparent the minute you meet him."

Sharpe did well in 2000, making a team-high 67 catches for five touchdowns. But he came through in a big way in the playoffs, when the struggling Ravens offense needed help. He grabbed a tipped ball and turned it into the key touchdown of Baltimore's first-round playoff win, a 21-3 victory over Denver.

The following week saw Sharpe come up with a big 56-yard catch that helped the Ravens score early and stay close in a 24-10 victory at Tennessee. Sharpe then turned a short pass on third and 18 into a 96-yard touchdown at Oakland as the Ravens rolled to a 16-3 victory in the AFC championship.

Sharpe had only one catch in the Super Bowl win over the Giants as he drew all kinds of attention from New York. But that coverage opened the door for Dilfer to throw to other players.

Sharpe broke the all-time record for receptions by a tight end the following year—set by Ravens GM Ozzie Newsome. The two celebrated together in a touching moment on the field.

A great sense of humor helped Sharpe become the leader in the Baltimore locker room. Sharpe loved to poke fun at everyone—including himself—and used his slick sense of humor to get points across in a nice way.

For example, when asked about Newsome, Sharpe said, "When I was growing up, I wanted to be Ozzie Newsome. I can't think of a better place to play, because I see the guy every single day. And he can see me every single day as I break his records."

That's what happened when Sharpe broke Newsome's record and became the NFL's all-time leader for receptions by a tight end—and both of them stood on the field and laughed. The Ravens didn't re-sign him after the 2001 season because of salary cap problems, and the team missed his leadership from the minute he left.

Matte's Musings on Shannon Sharpe

"He's a character in his own right. He's a funny guy. I remember him coming out to our radio show, and the restaurant was filled up, and Shannon said, 'I'm not signing any autographs. I ain't got time.' But he finally did it. My old philosophy and John Unitas's was that we're kind of public property. But guys don't want to be hounded. Shannon was funny. The motor-mouth. Everything he does, there's a strategy to it. He loves to be able to drop the words out there. He's a leader. If there's a guy who's ever in better condition, other than Ray or Jamal Lewis now, I don't know who he is. But the guy was a tremendous athlete. He watched what he ate. He watched what he drank. He was always physically fit and trying to stay healthy.

"I think he and Brian had a great relationship. Billick respected him because he was a worker. There was never a time that Shannon Sharpe didn't work. And he was always practicing and working hard—and then he came up with the big plays for him. Look at the playoffs in 2000. The Tennessee game, the Oakland game, those were big plays. He gave credit where credit was due. But the thing about Shannon is he backed them up, he caught the football, he made the big plays, he was a real leader on this team. The only thing I didn't understand was that he was very guarded about his personal life, which is fine and dandy and you can be that way, but when little kids come up, you've got to give them autographs. He just didn't like to do that. I'm not sure why. He had a presence about him. He had an air about him. But he was in tremendous condition all the time and still is in tremendous condition.

"Shannon commanded some respect. He was a veteran ballplayer who came in here and had two Super Bowl rings and had the credentials, and when you have credentials like he has, the younger players will respect that. And that's the way it should be. When I played, we'd make only four of five changes a year with players, but now they have wholesale changes because of free agency. But at least what's happening with free agents who are coming in who have credibility like a Shannon Sharpe, the respect is there for them. Billick brought him in and said here's your role, we want you to be a leader. And I think Shannon did a great job of carrying out his role. He made great plays and was getting to the receivers downfield and saying, hey, you have to block. Shannon was a complete football player. Now a player like Todd Heap leads by example. He's a very, very quiet guy, and Shannon pushed him. It made him a better football player. If you take a look down the line, and if Todd Heap plays the number of years that Shannon Sharpe does, then he'll have a great chance of going to the Hall of Fame because he catches that ball. He sacrifices his body. I saw him after some games with some bruises on his body, and he was just black and blue all over. He doesn't want to miss practice, and he doesn't want to miss games, because he enjoys it. Shannon made Todd sort of follow the footsteps. Todd wants to be good, and in the last couple of years, he's shown what kind of talent he has and what kind of respect he has among the league itself. This kid is a complete football player."

Shannon Sharpe brought playmaking skills and the swagger of a winner to the Ravens. (Photo by Phil Hoffmann)

Slow Start, Fast Finish

The signing of free agent wide receiver Marcus Robinson was looked upon as a possible big move before the 2003 season. After all, Robinson had been a solid receiver for Chicago before injuries slowed him.

But he truly struggled in his first games with the Ravens. Robinson was inactive in one game and made only seven catches through the first nine games as rookie quarterback Kyle Boller often looked for tight end Todd Heap or the running backs to throw the short quick passes that would neutralize the pass rushes and blitzes opposing teams kept throwing at the Ravens.

But things changed for Robinson when Wright stepped in at quarterback. The former South Carolina teammates clicked from the start. Robinson made 24 catches in the final seven games and became the team's go-to guy.

His big game came in the overtime victory against Seattle. Robinson made seven catches for 131 yards and a Ravens-record four touchdowns. He made touchdown catches of nine, 13, 25 and 50 yards to help the team rally from a 17-point fourth-quarter deficit.

Robinson finished with a total of 31 catches for 451 yards and six touchdowns, clearly delighting the Baltimore coaching staff. Billick was thrilled with Robinson's effort, especially in the Seattle game.

"It was great to see," Billick said. "Marcus needed a game to impact his confidence, and the team's confidence in him. You try to manufacture it as a coach. You work with the young man, but that is what Marcus needed, and [what] Anthony [Wright] needed. Hopefully, we can build on that. At the very least, the teams we will play as we go forward are going to have to look out there and at least half-consider what is going on the outside with Marcus Robinson running down the field."

Robinson is a quiet person who developed into a big-play receiver the team desperately needed. That's why the Seattle game proved to be a real jumping-off point. The smile he wore in the locker room was big enough to light up the stadium that day.

"Personally, I needed it big. I needed it very big," Robinson said. "Coming from Chicago, coming in here, knee surgery, back surgery, everybody's looking at [me being] injury-prone, things like that. And I started doubting myself for a minute. But I kept praying and I kept focusing. My wife kept praying for me. She kept pushing me and telling me, 'Marcus, you're the best receiver.' She would call and leave a message at every game: 'Marcus, you're the best receiver in the NFL.'"

Not Again

Orlando Brown was a locker room favorite during his first stint with the Ravens. The massive six-foot-seven, 350-pound tackle—with the nickname "Zeus"—made everyone laugh with his joking personality and combined with Ogden to give the Ravens a pair of towering offensive tackles.

But Brown sadly became best known for what happened when he went to the Cleveland Browns as a free agent in 1999. During the Browns' December 19 game with Jacksonville, official Jeff Triplette threw a penalty flag that accidentally struck Brown in the eye. What many people don't realize is those flags are weighted.

Brown always had worries about eye injuries, and being hit with the flag set him off. He shoved the official and was thrown out of the game. The NFL suspended him indefinitely after that. Combined with the eye injury, Brown found himself out of football for three years.

According to the Associated Press, Brown got an injury settlement with Cleveland the following year and wasn't fully cleared to play until before the 2003 season. His vision in that right eye still isn't 20-20, but he's dealing with it.

He had a good season with the Ravens in 2003 and eventually became the full-time starter after alternating with Ethan Brooks early on. Brown even played on the defensive side, helping stop the Seahawks in a crucial fourth-down play in the come-from-behind 44-41 victory. The Ravens became the NFL's top running team as Lewis racked up 2,066 yards.

But Brown's season ended on a poor note when he was called for two costly personal foul penalties in the team's 20-17 loss to Tennessee in the first round of the AFC playoffs. The last one pushed the Ravens back 15 yards before Dave Zastudil punted late in the fourth quarter of a 17-17 tie. The Titans got the ball in better field position and were able to drive for the game-winning field goal.

"Unfortunately, in the heat of the battle, things like that will happen," Billick said. "It's unfortunate; those things usually cost you like that.'

Brown said that he didn't want to be remembered only for those penalties. The five-year deal the Ravens signed him to during the off season should give him the opportunity to alter his legacy.

Ogden: Keeping It in the Family

Left tackle Jonathan Ogden has been a starter ever since he came to Baltimore as the No. 4 pick in the 1996 draft. He was the first player the Ravens ever picked in a draft. Later in the first round, the Ravens picked some linebacker named Ray Lewis.

The six-foot-nine, 340-pound Ogden has been a cornerstone of the Ravens' offensive line, and many consider him the NFL's best offensive lineman and one of the best of all time. He was picked for his seventh straight Pro Bowl in 2003. But

Ogden is different from many of the players in today's game because he doesn't seek attention for himself. He'll talk to the media and answer questions but is a low-key person who simply does his job and rarely looks for the spotlight that many of today's players seem to crave.

One of the things that many people don't know about is his extensive work with his younger brother Marques, a Howard University graduate whom Jacksonville made a late-round pick in the 2003 draft.

"It was just technique work primarily, just trying to get him to understand the technique you need to have when you came to this level, some of the things you can get away with at Howard that you couldn't get away with [here]," Jonathan said. "I was just trying to help him develop the finer points."

Marques Ogden is six years younger than Jonathan and started for most of his time at Howard. The Bison had to put him in different positions, as they weren't a very deep team offensively. He played center for the final six games of his senior year as injuries wiped out much of Howard's offensive line.

But he also worked hard with his older brother on how to play the game. Jonathan often tutored his six-foot-five, 300-pound sibling to teach him the little details about being a solid offensive lineman.

The two talked throughout the 2003 season as Marques tried to make his way on to the Jacksonville active roster while Jonathan made another Pro Bowl.

"I just tell him all the time, just continue to work hard," Jonathan said. "Just show them what you can do."

The New Tight End

Todd Heap came to the Ravens as a star. Literally.

When the HBO series *Hard Knocks* was being filmed during his rookie year when the Ravens were the defending Super Bowl champions, the cameras followed him everywhere.

And why not? He's six feet five, 252 pounds, with movie-star looks and Hall of Fame hands. He came to the Ravens as a late first-round draft choice anointed the team's star-to-be as a receiver.

But there were some tough things Heap had to deal with as a rookie in 2001. Heap first had to weather the storm of the opinionated Shannon Sharpe teaching him about life as an NFL tight end.

Heap also struggled through injuries during that first season after suffering a sprained ankle early in the year. The ankle problem sat him down for four games and also slowed him for much of the season. Heap finished with 16 catches and one touchdown that season.

But Heap stepped up in 2002 after salary cap problems prevented the Ravens from re-signing Sharpe. The tight end became the team's leading receiver with 68 catches for 836 yards and six touchdowns. His solid play earned him a Pro Bowl berth.

Heap became the only NFL tight end to lead his team in receiving and quickly showed why the Ravens were thrilled to get him so late in the first round of the 2001 draft—as many felt he'd be picked earlier.

"As far as tight ends go, you can't pass up a guy like Todd Heap," Sharpe said. "This guy is going to be in the top three or four in catching and yards for the next 10 years."

Heap was picked again for the Pro Bowl in 2003 despite the fact that the Ravens' passing game struggled all season. He finished with 57 catches for 693 yards and three touchdowns as Baltimore's passing attack had problems.

Teams repeatedly were double-teaming Heap, who wound up going for jump balls most of the time in the second half of the season. The Ravens rarely threw short passes or tosses over the middle to Heap like many tight ends got. He simply took what the team gave him and still made it to the Pro Bowl.

"I plan on going every year that I am playing," Heap said. "That is the expectation that I have. I plan on getting better every year, and as long as I can keep doing that, hopefully I can keep going."

Heap should have an expanded role in 2004 as Boller takes over once more as the starting quarterback. Boller often looked for Heap in 2003 before his injury and should likely find him many times again in an offense that will probably be more wide open since Jim Fassel has joined the coaching staff.

Many have seen and respected Heap's talent despite his low-key style. In this time where players often go through wild celebrations after making a catch, Heap simply shrugs that off.

"It's hard to get recognition without doing something crazy," Heap said. "People love that stuff. It's just not my style. Pointing first down after a five-yard catch? Maybe I'll get excited after a touchdown."

And that attitude suits Billick just fine.

"With no disrespect to Tony Gonzalez, Jeremy Shockey and Shannon Sharpe, and those are three players who are phenomenal talents, I wouldn't trade Todd for anybody," Billick said.

Matte's Musings on Todd Heap

"He's humble pie. He's the nicest young man, and he came into his own last year. You know, Woody Hayes had a saying—'I want quality boys.' If there's ever a quality kid who plays on this team, it's Todd Heap. He's a very good person who's conscious of his image. He's gotten married and is a great family guy, puts a lot back into the community and helps wherever he can.

"He knows he has a responsibility as an athlete to set an example. I think that the example that he's setting, well, I'd like my kids to look up to a Todd Heap. I don't think there's any higher compliment for an athlete to get than for a father to say, 'I want my son to grow up like you.' And that's the way I think people perceive Todd Heap. He's got the great hands and the great leaping ability. He gets his bell rung, but he keeps coming back. Todd's such a tough kid. He'll play hurt, and I've seen his body after the games and he's just black and blue. I mean, he's gotten shots in his shoulders, to his rib cage. He's just the complete player. He's too quiet to be the real leader. Todd just leads by example."

The Solid Fullbacks

The Ravens have taken advantage of solid play from two fullbacks during the Jamal Lewis years. Sam Gash and Alan Ricard became strong blockers who helped Lewis gain big yardage since he was picked in the first round of the 2000 draft.

Gash played a big role in the 2000 season. The former Pro Bowl fullback was a devastating blocker who helped Lewis have a great rookie season—and also helped then-Raven Priest Holmes do well. Gash's job didn't get a lot of publicity simply because of how little he touched the ball.

Lewis (1,364 yards rushing) and Holmes (588) helped Baltimore control the ball on offense for long stretches. Gash repeatedly helped the offensive lines open holes. He only ran the ball twice all season—gaining a total of two yards—and caught six passes for 30 yards and one touchdown.

Gash then played a similar role in 2001, helping with a team crippled by injuries to its running backs. Holmes left to go to Kansas City, while Jamal Lewis missed the entire season after suffering a knee injury in camp.

But Ricard slowly took over in 2002. He played in all 16 games and started eight of them, proving himself to be a strong blocker like Gash. But Ricard also showed he could do a little more with the ball.

He carried the ball 14 times for 58 yards and two touchdowns and also had 10 catches for 60 yards. The 2003 season saw Ricard rush for 79 yards and catch nine passes for 62 yards. Third-down back Chester Taylor saw some more playing time and contributed more, but Ricard's blocking often proved crucial.

"You have to be able to hit," Ricard said. "We have to get those guys up out of the hole for the running back. You have to be smart and pretty much know the scheme of things. Either you are going to hit a guy or you aren't."

And he usually did.

The Question Mark

Travis Taylor has done a lot of good things for the Ravens since they picked him in the first round of the 2000 draft. Taylor came to the team from Florida and was the 10th pick in the first round—the Ravens got him right after they picked Jamal Lewis in the first round.

But while Taylor has played very well at times, he's never quite burst into stardom. He's seemed on the verge of it a few times, but has never quite gotten there.

Injuries cut short his rookie year in 2000, and Taylor made 28 catches for 276 yards and three touchdowns. He added 42 catches for 560 yards and three scores in 2001. Taylor finally seemed to be finding his way when Jeff Blake stepped in for the injured Chris Redman after the first six games of 2002. Blake

Travis Taylor has delighted Ravens fans with acrobatic catches and frustrated them with inconsistent play. (Photo by Mitchell Layton)

truly seemed to be looking for Taylor, who finished with an impressive 68 catches for 869 yards and six touchdowns.

Blake loved to throw deep downfield, and Taylor loved to run patterns there. But things slid backwards in 2003 because the passing game was in the hands of inexperienced quarterbacks Kyle Boller and Anthony Wright—and the coaches wanted to stick more to the high-percentage passes.

Taylor finished with only 39 catches for 632 yards and three touchdowns, while again being plagued by some problems with dropped passes that bothered him at times throughout his first four seasons. The Ravens have been looking to him as the possible number one receiver since he joined the team.

The coaches always have respected him, with Billick saying nobody on the team is working harder than he is, and Taylor wanted to become a four-star receiver. It's just never quite happened.

"I've got to get to a point where I can demand the ball," Taylor said. "That's my next step. I think I can do that."

The question is where Taylor goes from here. The Ravens were looking at possibly bringing in other wide receivers for 2004, almost landing Terrell Owens, which would give Taylor a different role. Maybe being the No. 2 or 3 wide receiver would fit him better. Maybe it's the team's struggling passing game that's the problem.

Still, Taylor has shown the flashes of talent that leave the Ravens' staff hoping for more. The question is if he can finally break through.

Take It Easy, Jason

Simply put, Jason Brookins often drove his Ravens coaches crazy.

The Ravens had a big hole to fill at running back in the 2001 season after Jamal Lewis suffered a season-ending knee injury in training camp. Brookins made the coaches smile with his running ability but infuriated them with his attitude.

Brookins finished with 551 yards rushing plus five touchdowns that season, but battled injuries and numerous problems with the playbook and his weight.

Billick was constantly berating him for things like missing assignments and repeatedly not picking up blitzes and leaving quarterback Elvis Grbac open to being hit time and time again.

The Ravens then cut him the next spring after Brookins walked into mini-camp in poor shape. Green Bay signed him after that, and Brookins added another chapter to his story.

Brookins was running well with the Packers that summer in camp before coming up with his biggest mistake yet. One day, late in camp, someone asked Brookins to give the coaches his playbook for something.

Brookins got furious, thinking he was being cut and not understanding how that could happen because he'd been running so well throughout the summer. So he decided to do something about it.

He jumped in his car and took off, turned off the cell phone and basically made himself unreachable to the outside world for the next several hours. The Packers kept trying to find him but could not do it.

There was just one problem.

You see, the only thing the Packers wanted was to add something to his playbook. That's it. He thought he was being cut, so he just ran off. The Packers were not amused.

They cut him, and he hasn't been back to the NFL since.

Tony, Tony, Tony

The Ravens already had a solid left tackle when moving to Baltimore in 1996. Tony Jones had played very well for the Browns, but Baltimore had a chance to get Jonathan Ogden with its first pick in the 1996 draft.

The team picked Ogden, which upset Jones a little. Ogden was a natural left tackle, but Baltimore played him at left guard during his rookie season. Jones could read between the lines and saw that Ogden was going to be the starting left tackle at some point.

Jones made his feelings known in an article in Packer Plus online. Jones said that he wasn't all that sure he believed them.

"For right now, they are [keeping me at left tackle]," Jones said.

The Ravens liked having both players on the left side, and it really made for a tough blocking combination.

"We have to put our five best guys on the field," Newsome said at the time. "With Tony, we think we have one of the best left tackles in the game. So we feel good about our offensive line."

But the Ravens did change the following season, moving Ogden over to left tackle. However, Jones wasn't hurt too badly. He went to Denver and played on a couple of Super Bowl championship teams.

The Quiet Lineman

Edwin Mulitalo didn't get much notice when the Baltimore Ravens picked him in the fourth round of the 1999 draft.

The six-foot-three, 340-pound Mulitalo didn't even play until the sixth game that season—but an injury to right tackle Harry Swayne opened things up. Billick moved Everett Lindsay over to the right side and put Mulitalo at left guard, and he's pretty much been there ever since.

Mulitalo and left tackle Ogden make up a powerful left side of the line that has helped Jamal Lewis gain plenty of yards during his time in the NFL, and the pair played a big role in his record-breaking 2003 season.

Simply put, Mulitalo has developed into a solid offensive lineman. He's also been in Ogden's shadow a little bit, but his team certainly appreciates him.

"He is as solid a guard as there is in the league," Billick said. "He's not particularly demonstrative, and people don't care a lot about guards anyway. He's not boisterous, but he's started pretty much since the day he got here. And you get used to having him there all the time."

Mulitalo was behind the Festivus Maximus shirts and is one of the team's most popular players because of his great personality. He's always laughing, but when walking on to the field, Mulitalo becomes quite a different person.

The Ravens needed his physical power this season because the run became so important to their game. Mulitalo became a huge force—literally—on that line.

"Our job is to dominate, physically, the person in front of us," Mulitalo. "My job is to overpower the other guy, whether it's finesse or raw physical ability. So for me, yeah, I take it personally. Every time we establish the run, that's a symbol of our domination over the guy in front of us."

Mulitalo also was happy when signing a multiyear deal with the Ravens recently. He had wanted to stay with Baltimore, and the team saw him as valuable both on and off the field.

"It's something I've been dreaming about and working for, for pretty much all my big, 300-pound life," he said after the signing. "My wishes were met, and I'm just happy that my feelings were reciprocated. I'm excited to be here, and I'll be here for a long while."

Matte's Musings on Qadry Ismail and How Billick Pushes Buttons

"Qadry Ismail was a guy who could play. He was a wide receiver who had good hands. He'd go into a crowd and catch the ball, and once he caught the ball, he …could really run with [it]. I also thought Qadry was a class act. I would have thought about bringing Qadry back. He would come through for us. I'd have had a plane ready for him now.

"He and Billick had a good relationship. That's because Billick knows how to push the right buttons on people. Shula was the same way. Shula knew exactly how to motivate people, and you have to. You're dealing with 53 different personalities. What buttons do you push to make this guy go? Billick knows how to do that. He'll talk to his players, and he'll bring them in. He's got such a great rapport with his guy. He knows how to get the best efforts out of them. If you listen to Billick in a seminar where he's speaking to businessmen, you can totally relate. He gives examples of football and examples of business and parallels it. What he says makes sense. It just makes common sense. If you do steps one, two and three, step four is going to be a win situation for you. If you have customer relations and you make sure that you have on-time deliveries, if you do this, everything [works]. It's the same thing for football. If you prepare right, if you're in condition right and you execute right, what happens? You win football games.

"I think that Shula wasn't the silver tongue that Billick is now. Shula was very factual, very cut and straight, boom, boom, boom. He didn't elaborate. Billick has such a great command of the language. He's a dream for a reporter because he comes up with everything. He's the greatest orchestra leader in the world. If he wants to bring something to the forefront, he knows what buttons to push. I would have loved to have played for him because I could have lengthened my career. I would have been able to play a few more years longer. He would have been able to take advantage of what my abilities are and utilize me in the right way because he'd be calling the plays. When Unitas was in the huddle, John called his own plays. It's a different era now. It's a different time.

"We talked about the quarterback thing in the preseason. He said, 'What do you think?' He started talking, and I said, 'What do you think?' He said, 'I'm going with the kid,' and I said, 'I think you're making a mistake.' We were down on the field and talked for 20 minutes. We talked about it, and I said, 'You're putting a lot of responsibility on the young kid.' He said, 'I want to tell you how I feel.' He came to me and he brought it up. 'I really feel as a coach that right now if we go with this [quarterback], I think that he's going to progress quicker than Chris Redman, and that's why I'm going with him.' He knows I understand the game of football. I think he does respect what I do say. When I criticize on the radio, I criticize because they're making mistakes. And when I think they're right, I say they're right. I'm still upset with our receivers in 2003. They didn't do a damn thing in the first part of the year."

Chapter 9

A Cast of Thousands:
The Ravens' Quarterback Shuffle

The Quarterback Who Didn't Need to Score Much

Trent Dilfer received loads of criticism during his time with the Tampa Bay Bucs. He made too many mistakes, was too indecisive, couldn't throw the right ball, etc.

The bottom line—if anything went wrong with Tampa Bay, it seemed to be Dilfer's fault.

He came to the Ravens in 2000 pretty much expecting to be the backup quarterback for Tony Banks, another signal caller who had struggled in his career. Banks had a strong 1999 season as the Ravens finally reached .500 for the first time (8-8), and the team thought that 2000 might be its big playoff push.

But Banks found some of his old demons waiting for him early in 2000. He fumbled and threw interceptions, and the Baltimore offense began having all kinds of trouble. Everything fell apart during October, as the Ravens couldn't find a touchdown anywhere.

Banks threw five interceptions and no touchdowns during one three-game stretch, and Billick put in Dilfer late in a 14-6 loss to Tennessee in Baltimore. Dilfer appeared to throw a touchdown pass to Qadry Ismail in the final minutes, but the receiver was ruled out of the end zone.

Dilfer threw an interception in that game and another the following week, a 9-6 loss to Pittsburgh, which was the Ravens' fifth straight game without scoring a touchdown. But everything began to change the following week—Dilfer threw three touchdowns in a 27-0 rout of Cleveland.

Dilfer then threw two touchdowns the next week, as Baltimore became the first team ever to beat the Titans in Adelphia Coliseum. Even more impressive was how Dilfer beat the Titans—after his short pass was picked off by Perry Phenix and returned for an 87-yard touchdown, Tennessee had a 23-17 lead with 2:30 left.

But Dilfer led the Ravens 70 yards down the field and then threw a two-yard touchdown pass to Patrick Johnson in the front corner of the end zone with 25 seconds remaining, and Baltimore snuck away with a 24-23 victory.

"Early in your career, you tend to make a bigger deal out of [mistakes]," Dilfer said in a December 2000 article in *The Sporting News*. "As you go on, what you learn is you can play bad one week and light it up the next week. There's not a whole lot of carryover."

That win seemed to give the team a huge bolt of confidence. The Ravens then routed the Cowboys, Browns, and Chargers before sliding past the Cardinals in Dilfer's shakiest game. But they then beat the New York Jets, 34-20, despite giving up 524 yards total offense.

Dilfer then kept making plays throughout the playoffs, sparking the team to the four victories needed. He usually made one or two big plays per game—but the key was what he did not do.

Trent Dilfer understood how to win, and he helped bring the Lombardi Trophy back to Baltimore. (Photo by Phil Hoffmann)

He kept away from the costly and untimely mistakes. Dilfer finished with 12 touchdowns and 11 interceptions, but the pickoffs usually didn't hurt the team, whereas Banks's mistakes often came at the worst possible time.

Dilfer knew that the defense was so good that his job really was not to make mistakes and to score when the opportunity presented itself. He did that throughout the playoffs, finishing with three touchdown passes and just one interception.

He threw a 58-yard touchdown pass that broke open the 21-3 wild card win over Denver in the first playoff game. Dilfer then threw a 56-yard pass to Sharpe that set up an early touchdown in the 24-10 win at Tennessee the next week. He tossed a 96-yard touchdown pass to Sharpe that gave the Ravens control early in their AFC title game win over Oakland.

His biggest touchdown pass was a 38-yarder to Brandon Stokley midway through the first quarter in the Super Bowl that gave the Ravens a lead they never lost.

But the Ravens didn't re-sign the free agent after winning the title, a move that left many fans and critics scratching their heads—especially after the team signed free agent Elvis Grbac to a long-term deal and he had problems from the start.

Dilfer became a type of folk hero in Baltimore, especially after he left. How the team could not re-sign a quarterback who led them to a Super Bowl win was the question many asked, especially after Grbac struggled so badly the following year. Dilfer refused to say much negative about the Ravens, although he clearly felt some anger toward Billick and how he was treated after winning the title. But Dilfer wouldn't get into it and quietly moved on.

The irony—when Seattle came back to Baltimore during the 2003 season, Dilfer was a backup and got in for one play in overtime of the Ravens' 44-41 win. But he couldn't do anything to pay back the Ravens, who went on to victory.

The Quarterback Controversy

No one ever really knew the story behind the quarterback derby that the Ravens had in 2003. And no one ever really expected it to end the way that it did.

Everything started with the Ravens using their second first-round pick to take California quarterback Kyle Boller. The team had actually tried to trade up to pick quarterback Byron Leftwich after Minnesota bungled its first-round pick, but when trying to work out a trade, they couldn't get through because the line was busy.

The poor phone service put the Ravens in a tough spot. Jacksonville took Leftwich, and the Ravens picked Terrell Suggs with their first pick, the 10th overall. They then quickly swung a trade with New England that gave the Pats Baltimore's second-round choice that day and a first-round pick in 2004, which let them pick Boller 19th overall.

The Ravens were both shocked and delighted to get two four-star players in the first round, but the spotlight quickly fell on Boller.

Many have felt that Billick always wanted a quarterback who could go deep, something the Ravens never really had under his watch. Tony Banks and Elvis Grbac were the closest things to it, but both kept turning the ball over.

The Ravens said that there'd be a competition in training camp between Boller and Chris Redman. But Boller came in late after a holdout, and Redman got an early jump and looked good in preseason games. However, Boller quickly made up ground and won the starting job.

Some critics said that Billick never had any intention of giving the job to Redman because Boller was exactly what the coach wanted. But no matter what happened, Boller started the season and struggled from the beginning—especially with the speed of the game.

"That part of the game will be the biggest adjustment for me," Boller said. "Everyone says it—the speed, the speed. But the game will slow down for me once I've been through everything, once I have run all these plays, faced all these teams."

Boller slowly began to find his way toward the midpoint of the season before hurting a muscle in his quadriceps late in the first half of the November 9 loss at St. Louis. Surgery sidelined him for the next month, and he saw action in a only handful of plays after that as Billick left backup Anthony Wright in to run the team.

Boller had to take a lot of criticism for his mistakes. He completed 116 of 224 passes for 1,260 yards with seven touchdowns and eight interceptions, but his turnovers seemed to keep coming at the wrong times. However, he was clearly growing as the season went on.

Redman had a poor game when coming in for him against St. Louis, and Billick went to Wright as the starter after that. The former Dallas backup had some up-and-down stretches and completed 94 for 178 for 1,199 yards with nine touchdowns and eight interceptions. He showed a tendency for fumbling also, but Wright made a number of clutch plays that helped the Ravens to the AFC North title.

"Anthony would be the first to say it's an ongoing process," offensive coordinator Matt Cavanaugh said. "You never come out of a game and say, 'I've got it figured out.' We knew he was a strong-armed, athletic quarterback who was smart."

Wright's leadership abilities also impressed the Ravens. The team rallied around him, starting with the come-from-behind 44-41 victory over Seattle when his wife was ready to deliver a baby.

"This is something you dream of," Wright said after that game. "It's unbelievable—down by that much and to come back. It gives me tears."

Wright then started the rest of the season and into the playoffs. The Ravens were left with an interesting choice at season's end. They had to decide whether to re-sign Wright and what to do with him. Boller was healthy and said he considered himself the starter.

Billick said that Boller would be the starter, and Wright then signed a two-year contract in March. There would be no quarterback derby in 2004, but the Ravens were comfortable with a backup who knew the system and how to play the game.

Matte's Musings on Boller's Rookie Season

"Well, there were a lot of dropped balls, and the rookie quarterback hadn't learned to read defenses yet. A lot of people criticized Boller, but I see that he is going to be the player of the future. You saw the guts and determination that he brings. I think he's got a spark. He's sort of a hurry-up kind of guy. I think he's got capabilities of rising to the occasion, but it's just like a running back. If you don't have the offensive line in front of you, you're not going to do very well. Also, if you don't have wide receivers who can catch the ball and who can get open, then you're going to be branded as a quarterback who can't get the job done. I think there's some responsibility on the coaching staff now to have some game plan that's conducive to passing. Find the dead spots. Find the hook spots. You take a look at Marshall Faulk on the Rams, Edgerrin James of the Colts, Priest Holmes with Kansas City. Good Lord, he's making a living out of doing that. I caught 40 or 50 balls coming out of the backfield every year. Let's say that I get five or six yards, and then you've got a second and four. That's better for the offense. The Ravens have got to mix it up a little bit on passing. They have to do that. They've got to be able to get everyone involved. Let me tell you, as a rookie, it's really hard. As a rookie, I should have been cut. There's so many different defenses that they're throwing at Boller. You have to be able to pick up your keys, and that's hard to do as a rookie.

Ravens fans hope that Kyle Boller will bring some consistency to the quarterback position. (Photo by Mitchell Layton)

"What Boller has to do is keep working on things like taking some film home and studying, and he should come in here to Baltimore and work with the offensive coaches and the pass receiving coaches and sit with the defensive coaches and ask questions. What are they going to do against me here? I was very fortunate because I played on defense also, and I understood what they were trying to do. Coaches have got to sit down with this kid and pound it into him. You have to spend 80 percent of your time studying and 20 percent of it getting in condition. You have to study, and you really get proficient at reading defenses. It's boring as hell and it ain't easy, but you have to do it. You sit down with those coaches and study. You ask for the keys. You want to know what they're doing. Bill Belichick or the offensive coordinator in New England really worked with quarterback Tom Brady on the keys. He knows what to look for and when to look for it. And he also has the sense to pull it back in if nothing's there.

"I really see a breakout season for Boller in 2004. I really think he's going to spend a lot of time studying and looking at what he did wrong. He's got to put the time in if he wants to be a great quarterback. Boller's got a great attitude, and I really like it a lot. You have to stand up and be accounted for, and if you screw up in a game, say hey, I ain't perfect, but I'm going to learn from my mistakes.

"That is what he has to do now. I think that's what's going to happen. Boller really was getting better as the season went along. I think he's going to come out of the blocks a hell of a lot better in 2004. Anthony Wright learned a lot also when stepping in to play. I thought that, under the circumstances, he stepped up and did a great job. He made some bad plays, but he really played well many times."

A Short Stint at QB

When Billick took over in 1999, he quickly turned to quarterback Scott Mitchell to spark his offense. But there were questions about Mitchell from the start.

The big left-hander had a great arm, no question about that, but he'd only had certain amounts of success in Detroit and came to a rebuilding Baltimore team in 1999. Billick spent the preseason going out of his way to show confidence in Mitchell, who threw fairly well that summer.

But everything fell apart pretty quickly once the season started. Mitchell played poorly in Billick's first game, a 27-10 loss to a St. Louis team that many thought wasn't very good. They went on to win the Super Bowl that season, so the geniuses were wrong.

Mitchell then struggled badly in the second game and got pulled early, and the Ravens eventually went to Tony Banks at quarterback—who had a career year.

Mitchell was never really heard from in Baltimore again.

The Mad Bomber

Vinny Testaverde was the Ravens' first quarterback. He scored the franchise's first touchdown and was probably the most recognizable player in the opening year.

Testaverde had been considered a bit of a disappointment during his first nine years in the league—throwing more touchdowns than interceptions just twice. But everything came together in Baltimore in 1996.

The Ravens began throwing the long ball with more and more regularity as the season went on. They had to because the defense was giving up points by the barrel. Testaverde had the best season of his career, completing 325 of 549 passes for 4,177 yards with a career-best 33 touchdowns and only 19 interceptions to earn a spot in the Pro Bowl.

But Testaverde did show one disturbing trend, something that had bothered him throughout his career—the tendency to throw interceptions at the wrong time. It cost the Ravens several times that year. But it didn't turn out to be that big a deal because Baltimore finished with a 4-12 record and wasn't a playoff contender.

The interception problem reared its head in a bad way the following year. Testaverde finished with 18 touchdowns and 15 interceptions. He completed 271 of 470 passes for 2,971 yards and lost his starting job late in the season to Eric Zeier, the backup quarterback.

Testaverde quickly lost some of his popularity in Baltimore. People began to call for Zeier to get playing time as the team stumbled following a 3-1 start. The Ravens finished with a 6-9-1 record, and that ended Testaverde's career with the team. He moved on to the Jets and found some good success there.

Interestingly, he came back to Baltimore during the final game of the 2000 season as the Ravens were hot and in the midst of their Super Bowl run. Testaverde helped the Jets run up over 500 yards of offense that day, but McAlister's 98-yard interception return for a touchdown late in the first half helped the Ravens turn things around and go on to a 34-20 victory.

Elvis Has Left the Building

The signing of Elvis Grbac was one of the most controversial moves that the Baltimore Ravens ever made, for a variety of reasons.

Fans and some in the media couldn't understand why the team wouldn't re-sign Trent Dilfer, the quarterback who started as the team won the Super Bowl in 2000. But team officials reportedly doubted that Dilfer could pull it off again.

Some experts felt the defense carried the team in a way that hadn't really been seen before and the offense got lucky at times. Dilfer really struggled, completing just five passes in the playoff game against Tennessee, but Sharpe turned one into a long gain that set up a touchdown, and the defense scored one touchdown while the special teams got another in a 24-10 victory.

Most felt, when the Ravens decided not to bring back Dilfer, that they'd go to free agent Brad Johnson, who'd been down the road in Washington. Johnson played under Billick at Minnesota and clearly still liked him.

During an interview the previous spring while playing with the Redskins, I happened to bring up that I was from Baltimore, and Johnson's face just lit up.

"How's Brian, how's he doing, he's just great," Johnson said with a smile.

But the Ravens were trying to decide between Johnson and Grbac and reportedly offered both similar contracts. Johnson then signed a long-term deal with Tampa Bay, and Grbac came to Baltimore to be the team's starter.

Grbac got off to a good start, looking solid in training camp, but everything fell apart early in the regular season. He threw 63 passes in a shocking 21-10 loss at Cincinnati during the second game of the season, and some thought they saw him with a tear running down his face, which raised all kinds of controversy in town.

Grbac kept making mistakes, throwing interceptions and looking spooked in the pocket. Randall Cunningham was waiting on the bench, and Billick absolutely refused to go to him until Grbac was injured.

The problems got worse during the season after the Ravens stumbled to a 3-3 start. The Ravens needed to win several close games and didn't lock up a playoff spot until beating Minnesota, 19-3, on the final Monday night of the season in a game rescheduled because of the September 11th tragedy.

Anthony Wright stepped into the starting lineup and guided the Ravens to the 2003 AFC North Division title, the first in Ravens' history. (Photo by Mitchell Layton)

But in that final game, the Ravens were trying to be so careful with their offense that it looked like a carbon copy of the year before when they let Dilfer throw only in selected spots.

The players were almost openly and blatantly criticizing Grbac in several spots—especially tight end Sharpe, who kept making references to the fact that the quarterback was brought in to do a job and wasn't getting it done. Billick worked at banning internal criticism of Grbac and the offense.

Grbac looked much better in the 20-3 playoff win over the Dolphins in Miami. But everything fell apart in an AFC semifinal at Pittsburgh. The Steelers' ferocious pass rush clearly bothered Grbac from the start, and the offense couldn't do much in the 27-10 loss.

The Ravens still tried to bring Grbac back in the off season, but offered him a large pay cut. Baltimore then basically didn't pick up the option, and Grbac walked away from football after a very painful final season.

Grbac finished by completing 265 of 467 for 3,033 yards with 15 touchdowns and 18 interceptions plus a shaky quarterback rating of 71.1. The playoffs were even worse. He had just one touchdown and three interceptions and never found his way.

The Quarterback Question

When Billick came to Baltimore in 1999, people felt that they'd finally be getting some kind of efficient passing offense because many felt he was a type of offensive genius, having helping turn the Vikings into one of the league's best.

But quarterbacks actually have been Billick's biggest problem since coming to Baltimore. Here's a list of those who've started for Billick: Anthony Wright, Kyle Boller, Scott Mitchell,

Stoney Case, Tony Banks, Trent Dilfer, Elvis Grbac, Randall Cunningham, Chris Redman, Jeff Blake.

Several seemed to have good chances at being successful. Mitchell, Banks, Grbac, Cunningham and Blake all started before in the NFL with some degree of success. But each struggled and faced some kind of negative.

For example, Grbac's problems were made worse by the fact that starting running back Jamal Lewis was knocked out for the season for a training camp knee injury. Plus, several running backs also were sidelined with injuries that season, often forcing the Ravens to pass more than they liked.

Blake took over in midseason and worked with an inexperienced crew of receivers. Redman had the same problem and never started an NFL game before beginning the 2002 season as the team's No. 1 quarterback.

But inexperience at quarterback caused even more problems at that position. Case had very little NFL on-field time. Boller started the 2003 season as a rookie, while Wright had appeared in only six games—starting five—before taking over the No. 1 job midway through the season.

Cunningham was on his final NFL legs, at age 38, and not quite the quarterback he once was with Philadelphia and the Vikings, when coming to Baltimore to back up Grbac in 2001. He looked good from time to time when playing, but Baltimore fans kept thinking of his younger days, adding to the pressure mounting on Grbac.

The question now is whether Boller can become what the Ravens are hoping for. It would quiet the quarterback controversies for a long time.

Matte's Musings
on the Quarterback Question

"Dilfer was a meat and potatoes type of quarterback. He wasn't fancy, and Billick was smart enough to know what his capabilities were, which were the short passes. He kept the offense pretty basic. But [Trent] was a spark plug. He was a leader out there and was always hustling. There was always a sense of urgency when he was quarterbacking. He made the team move, and I like that in an athlete.

"I saw a couple of things just recently when we were behind Cincinnati, and nobody hustled, there was no sense of urgency. That's something Kyle Boller's got to learn as a quarterback. He's got to learn what a sense of urgency is. He's got to get his team up to the line of scrimmage and say, 'Hey, let's go, guys, let's go, let's hurry up and get up and in position.' We wasted eight or 10 seconds by struggling up to the line of scrimmage.

"That's what Dilfer did. He brought stability to the offense. It wasn't fancy. It wasn't flamboyant. He just had guys out there with the ability to catch the football. I just thought he did a great job of quarterbacking, and to see him leave the next year was very disappointing to me. Billick knew he had to improve the offense, which I could understand, but [letting] this guy go surprised me. I thought he did a great job here for the team. As far as Tony Banks earlier that year, I played for a quarterback who liked to throw the football too, but he was smart enough to use the running game to enhance the passing game. Banks was the kind of guy, in my estimation, who just liked to throw the football. That's why he's bouncing all over the place. You can't blame it all on Banks, though. Coaches call the plays; the guys up in the sky are saying what they think they ought to go with. But Dilfer just went out there and got the job done and didn't make the big mistakes, didn't fumble the ball, didn't throw the interception, didn't make the big mistakes. He had a lot of hustle and a lot of spirit. I thought he was a great asset to this ball club and one of the reasons why they won. But then, boom, he's gone. They want to start somebody else.

"Grbac just didn't fit here. He didn't look like he was into the game all the time. It was a little like he was going through the motions. Grbac was not the answer. That's for sure. He was a big, strong kid who could throw the ball, that's for sure. He just didn't click with this team at all. You have to have chemistry to be able to play with a team. Guys used to come in and take a look at me and think, look at that slow fat little halfback over here, but my chemistry with Johnny Unitas and my chemistry with the coaching staff was so great because they knew that I knew the game better than anybody else. The only thing that kept me alive in the National Football League was that I was smart enough to understand what was going on. Unitas always said that he knew where Tom Matte was going to be on every play. Grbac just didn't click. He didn't have that chemistry with his own players. Hey, it happens. He was a loner and kind of isolated himself from the team.

"But with Boller, they brought him along pretty slowly before he got hurt. I could see a progression with Kyle Boller even from the beginning of the season, and he's a tough kid. But again, he's got to be able to have that leadership, he's got to be able to earn that respect, and I think he did so. I think that Ray Lewis summed it up after the game in Cincinnati when the kid got hurt, and he liked how Boller wouldn't come off the field. He said, 'I'm all right, I'm all right, I'm all right.' It's a long season, and rookies don't understand what 20 games are all about. That's two full seasons for a rookie, for a college kid. He could have gotten burned out towards the end of the season, but he was doing well.

"I don't think Banks wanted to take the responsibility. Here's the thing—if you're a leader, you're going to step up and assume responsibility no matter what the coaches call. Did I execute the play properly, or did I not execute the play properly? I think that's where leadership comes to the forefront—do you assume that responsibility. We worked on these plays. The coaches think it's going to work, now I have to execute it and make it happen. I have to run the play. Now there are some times when the defense is good and they're going to screw it up and it ain't going to work. But if it's an interception and it's thrown into double coverage, that's my fault. I shouldn't be throwing the ball into double coverage. Even though we practice all week on it; we didn't anticipate that defense. You've got to identify it and read it and then go to your next choice. You have a progression of choices, one, two, three. They try to keep them in line so that you're not turning your head to the left, to the right and back to the left and the right. What they try to do is give you a progression of receivers to watch and to check down to. And they try to make it easy for him.

"Dilfer was smart enough to be able to read. He'd been around the league long enough [that] instead of taking any chances, he'd tuck it away and either take the sack or run the ball. He stayed away from making mistakes. He didn't make the big mistakes. If you take a look at the turnover ratio for the drive to the Super Bowl, they had a plus ratio. The thing that I was impressed with was that he had that spark of leadership that this team needed. He pulled them together. I don't think Dilfer thought of himself as a great athlete. He'd say, 'I'm not the greatest athlete in the world, but I'm going to give you everything I've got.' That's the way I played as a player. I didn't have all the athletic ability in the whole wide world. But when I was on that field, I was thinking all the time. I was making sure if the ball was thrown to me, I was going to catch it. I was making sure I was going to cover that ball up if I was in traffic. I tried to be consistent. I'd come back into the huddle and Unitas would say to me, 'What have you got?' and I'd better damn well have it.

"I think there was good communication [between] the players and the coaches [and] Dilfer, and he was always willing to learn. I think he showed that. I think he probably did know he wasn't going to be coming back. Billick was looking for something special. He wanted a guy who could throw the ball and open it up. Dilfer commanded that respect. He was taking them through a hell of a season. The offense didn't always do that much, but they didn't make the big mistakes, and that's where you have to give credit to Dilfer. They knew they had a great defense [that] would get the field position for them. They'd make a couple of big plays every damn game for them, and as Ray Lewis said, 'If you give me 10 points, we'll win.' They had such confidence in their defense. We had a great defense in 1968 and 1970 with the Colts. Get us a couple of touchdowns and we'll win the game, that's how we thought."

Chapter 10

SPECIAL TEAMS

Life Is Just a Kick

Matt Stover is the only player left on the Ravens who has been with the team since it moved from Cleveland.

He's also something unusual. Stover is one of the most accurate kickers in NFL history, but in a day when many players are desperately seeking attention, he just focuses solely on doing his job.

"I've learned to go one game at a time and see where we end up," Stover said. "When my focus gets too long, my world gets too big, and it becomes cumbersome for me, and I just can't handle it very well. So I just go, 'Hey, we've got this team this week.' I don't even know who we play after that."

Stover's solid focus has helped him in a number of ways throughout his career. He's made 321 of 391 field goal attempts (82.1 percent), including a typical 33-for-38 effort during the 2003 season.

Matt Stover is the longest-tenured Raven and often the best scoring threat during the Super Bowl season. (Photo by Mitchell Layton)

Billick thinks very highly of Stover and this past season also helped him by bringing in Wade Richey to handle the kickoff chores and assist in a few very long field goal attempts.

But the relationship between the player and coach has come a very long way since Billick took over in 1999.

Stover struggled a bit at the start of the 1999 season. The new coach was a bit worried when Stover made only 10 of his first 15 field goals as the Ravens were trying to become a winning team for the first time.

So Billick brought in people to work out during the week during the season. Stover knew it, but that didn't affect him. In fact, it seemed to make him even better.

Stover took off after the slow start and made his final 18 field goals, including a 50-yard kick as time ran out to give the Ravens a 34-31 victory over Cincinnati on November 21. That kick helped him earn AFC Special Teams Player of the Week honors.

At season's end, Billick made it very clear that he had learned some things about Stover.

"At the end of my first season, reporters asked what had I learned and what would I do differently," Billick said later on. "I would have worked with Matt differently. I gained considerable respect for him as I watched how hard he worked to prepare."

Stover had some trouble in the team's early years in Baltimore, missing some big kicks, but that seemed to change as time went on.

The kicker nearly carried the Baltimore offense at times throughout the 2000 season when the Ravens went five games without scoring a touchdown. He made 35 of 39 field goal attempts and led the NFL with 135 points that year and earned his first Pro Bowl berth.

Stover kept going after that and played a similar role during 2003 as the team's offense sputtered for much of the season. He finished with the aforementioned 33-for-38 effort and kept making big field goals.

One of the biggest was the overtime kick that gave the Ravens the wild come-from-behind victory over Seattle—and Stover's reaction told a lot about his personality and why he's so valuable to the team.

"Well, that's what I live for," Stover said. "This team did a great job getting us into field goal position and never gave up. And what are you going to do? I went out there and did my job. That's what they pay me for. I got a good snap and a good hold on both of them. I've got good guys around me, and then the next thing you know, we win a ballgame."

Your Path Is Blocked

Ed Reed showed in his first two years that he's going to become one of the top defensive backs in the NFL. He earned his first Pro Bowl berth in his second year—some thought he also should have gotten one as a rookie in 2002—and showed an amazing ability to simply make plays.

Reed finished by tying a team record with seven interceptions this season, including one in the season finale against Pittsburgh. But Reed does one other thing that's just as valuable, if not more.

The former Miami star has shown an amazing ability to block punts. Baltimore had never had a blocked punt in the first six years of the franchise until Reed did it against Denver early in the team's third game of 2002.

That was one of the key plays of the season as the Ravens had stumbled to an 0-2 start and were underdogs against a strong Broncos team in a *Monday Night Football* game. But Reed's blocked punt put the Ravens on the Denver 13 and set

Ed Reed is a great safety, but he also has an incredible talent for blocking punts. (Photo by Mitchell Layton)

up a Jamal Lewis score that gave Baltimore a 14-3 lead. The Ravens went on to a 31-point second quarter and a win.

Reed did it again later in the season against Tennessee. He blocked a Craig Hentrich punt, picked up the loose ball and ran for an 11-yard touchdown that helped the Ravens to a 13-12 victory over the Titans.

He blocked a punt and returned it for a 22-yard touchdown that sparked Baltimore's win over Arizona in 2003. It was a turning point in the game.

"I've been doing that since high school," Reed said. "It's just a matter of getting to the ball. I'm going to get to the ball. Once the ball is snapped, I'm going to follow it."

Life Is Just a Snap

The Ravens have turned many heads with their willingness to do things that some would consider unusual simply to get good players.

Baltimore drafted punter David Zastudil with its first pick in the fourth round of the 2002 draft. Teams have shied away from using a draft pick on a punter—unless he's Ray Guy—in recent years. But the Ravens don't want to worry about having a carousel of players going through their front door every year.

That's another reason why they picked long snapper Joe Maese in the sixth round of the 2001 draft. Maese played for New Mexico, where he never was on scholarship but made himself into one of college football's best long snappers.

He's now played with the Ravens for three years and turned out to be a very consistent snapper, making almost no mistakes and getting players and coaches one less thing to worry about.

Maese truly has a tough job where mistakes are noticed most and become costly. The six-foot, 241-pound Maese understands exactly what comes with his job.

"It's a lot of pressure because I realize that if it wasn't for snapping, I wouldn't be around here," he said. "It's one of those things where you have to be almost perfect. Every snap has to be perfect. The only snaps they remember are the ones that are bad."

Maese will do about 75-100 snaps on Wednesdays and Thursdays in season—splitting between punts and field goals—while doing 50-75 on Fridays.

"The thing is, I've done it so many times, you don't even think about [mistakes]," Maese said. "You just [snap] the ball."

Maese said the longer he's with the Ravens and in the NFL, the more comfortable he becomes. He's had to fight off people going for his job on several occasions—and just shrugs it off because that's something that comes with the territory.

Maese works just as hard in the off season, snapping three or four days a week with some other snappers he knows in the Phoenix area. He's established now and simply wants to keep doing what he's been dong.

"You know what to expect more every year," Maese said. "In my rookie year, I didn't know what to expect. You just try to stay in the same routine because it's worked so far. You just practice and it becomes muscle memory."

A Bad Break

A few days after the Ravens edged Pittsburgh in overtime in the finale of the 2003 season, Zastudil was still hearing the jokes.

"Did you see those articles comparing him to Dick Butkus?" Maese asked with a laugh.

Zastudil simply rolled his eyes and grinned. The lanky punter never did much to call attention to himself, but that's exactly what happened during the 13-10 overtime win over Pittsburgh.

He made a great diving tackle on Antwaan Randle-El late in the first half that might have saved a touchdown. But the tackle came at a cost as Zastudil broke his nose and suffered a concussion.

"I just went full speed to hit him and his elbow [hit] me," Zastudil said. "I just remember colliding with him. I watched it on film."

Zastudil said he was really stunned by the hit and went into a fog for several minutes.

"I went out and had a 10- to 15-minute period where I was out of it," he said. "I went back out and sat on the bench and I was in a daze and they said, hey, hold off for a minute."

Zastudil tried to punt and got off a weak 27-yard kick the first time the Ravens had to punt in the third quarter, and the doctors told him that was all for a while. But when Baltimore had to punt a few minutes later, they ran into trouble because of some NFL rules.

Third-string quarterback Chris Redman is actually listed as the backup punter. But because he was officially named as the third-string quarterback, he couldn't go in to punt at that point. So Billick went to Kyle Boller.

The young quarterback had to punt from deep in Ravens territory and got off a decent 29-yard kick. Maese said they knew Boller would kick if Zastudil still was a little fuzzy, and the two actually worked out together during the halftime break—so Boller was as ready as he could be for the task.

Zastudil came back after that, getting off punts of 42 and 43 yards. He did even better in the Tennessee loss the following week, blasting several long punts that helped the Ravens in the field-position battle. He finished with an AFC-best average of nearly 49 yards per punt.

And his nose was just fine afterwards.

"It's just part of the game," Zastudil said. "Sometimes you hit a better punt, a better direction sometimes and you don't have to deal with those plays."